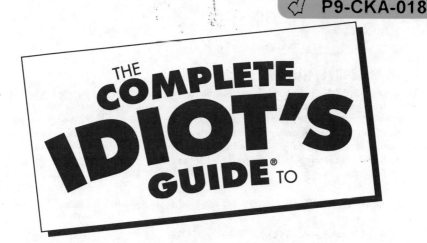

THE COMPLETE IDIOT'S GUIDE® TO

Dog Health and Nutrition

by Margaret Bonham and James M. Wingert, D.V.M.

ALPHA

A Pearson Education Company

Copyright © 2003 by Margaret Bonham

International Standard Book Number: 0-02-864455-7
Library of Congress Catalog Card Number: 2002115727

04   03   02   8   7   6   5   4   3   2   1

Interpretation of the printing code: The rightmost number of the first series of numbers is the year of the book's printing; the rightmost number of the second series of numbers is the number of the book's printing. For example, a printing code of 02-1 shows that the first printing occurred in 2002.

Printed in the United States of America

Note: This publication contains the opinions and ideas of its authors. It is intended to provide helpful and informative material on the subject matter covered. It is sold with the understanding that the authors and publisher are not engaged in rendering professional services in the book. If the reader requires personal assistance or advice, a competent professional should be consulted.

The authors and publisher specifically disclaim any responsibility for any liability, loss, or risk, personal or otherwise, which is incurred as a consequence, directly or indirectly, of the use and application of any of the contents of this book.

For marketing and publicity, please call: 317-581-3722

The publisher offers discounts on this book when ordered in quantity for bulk purchases and special sales.

For sales within the United States, please contact: Corporate and Government Sales, 1-800-382-3419 or corpsales@pearsontechgroup.com

Outside the United States, please contact: International Sales, 317-581-3793 or international@pearsontechgroup.com

Publisher: *Marie Butler-Knight*
Product Manager: *Phil Kitchel*
Managing Editor: *Jennifer Chisholm*
Senior Acquisitions Editor: *Mike Sanders*
Development Editor: *Michael Thomas*
Production Editor: *Billy Fields*
Copy Editor: *Catherine Schwenk*
Illustrator: *Chris Eliopoulos*
Cover/Book Designer: *Trina Wurst*
Indexer: *Tonya Heard*
Layout/Proofreading: *Angela Calvert, John Etchison*

Contents at a Glance

Contents

Appendixes

Foreword

The Pet Food Institute has estimated that in 2001 there were over 60 million pet dogs and 75 million pet cats in the United States. It has been further estimated that the majority of households in this country have at least one cat or dog. The benefits of pet ownership are tremendous. Those of us who have chosen to include a pet in our family will probably live longer and happier lives as a result of that decision. Dogs, in particular, bring us pleasure each and every day. What other family member is at the door every time you come home, wagging their tail and greeting you as if you had been gone for days and they missed you the entire time you were away? Dogs just enjoy being with us and they seem to thank us daily for allowing them the privilege of being part of our family.

In order to enjoy and gain the full effect of this wonderful relationship, there are obligations we must accept. We are the caregivers for our four-legged companions. We decide when they eat, sleep, and exercise. Their health and well-being are totally under our control. Their quality of life is directly related to our ability to care for their needs.

The Complete Idiot's Guide to Dog Health and Nutrition, by Margaret Bonham and Dr. James M. Wingert, is an excellent resource for establishing a plan to provide your pet with the very best care.

The book stresses the importance of prevention rather than waiting for trouble to occur. Finding the right veterinarian is essential. The American Veterinary Medical Association estimates that there are approximately 65,000 veterinarians in the United States. The authors give sound advice on how to choose the right one. Veterinarians are advocates for the welfare of your pet. With your help, the veterinarian will establish a routine preventive regimen that will assure the health and quality of life you expect for your friend.

The Complete Idiot's Guide to Dog Health and Nutrition lists all of the health issues one must consider in caring for a pet. Vaccinations, spaying/neutering, grooming, heartworm prevention, deworming, flea and tick control, and tattooing or microchipping are all discussed in detail. The importance of regular exercise also is stressed.

There is a very basic discussion of some of the more common diseases and conditions that sometimes occur. The description of symptoms is a wonderful resource for helping you identify and report concerns to your veterinarian early in the course of the disease. Early detection of a problem enables your veterinarian to have the best chance of resolving the problem quickly and completely.

Nutrition is essential, and quality nutrition—along with exercise and good veterinary care—are the hallmarks of a long and healthy life for your companion.

Today we are all concerned about our own health and well-being. As a result, there is a movement in this country towards a more natural or holistic approach to life and, in particular, diet. As one searches for the same nutritional benefits for our dogs, it quickly becomes apparent that there is a lot of confusing information out there on the Internet and on paper. It seems that everyone has an opinion on the best diets for our best friends.

Margaret Bonham and Dr. Wingert take great pains to discuss many misconceptions about the best diet for your pet. After reading this book, you will have a clear understanding of the advantages and disadvantages of the many forms of nutrition popular today. Homemade diets, raw or BARF (Bones And Raw Foods) diets, dry dog foods, canned foods, and other forms of nutrition are all evaluated. Better yet, there is a detailed discussion on how to read the labels of commercially prepared foods—what the label says and what it does not say and how to get the information necessary in order to choose the right diet for your pet.

After reading this book, you will have a better understanding of the basics of caring for your pet. You will also have a wonderful resource that you will refer back to on numerous occasions. There is a wealth of information condensed into a concise and logical format that makes it easy to review particular sections when necessary.

For further information, don't forget the appendixes. There is a listing of organizations, periodicals, and books, which will be invaluable in furthering your knowledge on a specific subject.

Dogs give us so much each and every day. It is our responsibility to give back in the form of loving care and advocacy. *The Complete Idiot's Guide to Dog Health and Nutrition* will give you the knowledge and resources to assure a long, healthy, and happy life for your beloved dog.

Albert S. Townshend, D.V.M.
Staff Veterinarian, Eagle Pet Products, Inc.
www.Eaglepack.com

Dr. Townshend has had his own small animal practice for over thirty years. He was a contributing author to the veterinary text *Canine Sports Medicine and Surgery*. Recently he has become the staff veterinarian for Eagle Pet Products, Inc., a small quality manufacturer of pet foods. His interests include canine sports medicine; in particular, as it relates to nutrition.

He was instrumental in forming the International Sled Dog Veterinary Medical Association and served as the secretary/treasurer for many years. He has been a volunteer trail veterinarian for the famous Iditarod Sled Dog Race and many other races throughout North America.

Introduction

In this book, you'll learn all about the basics of dog health care and nutrition. You'll learn how to find the right vet and how to recognize problems before things get out of hand. You'll learn the basics of good nutrition and how to decipher the mumbo jumbo on the dog food label. What's more, you'll learn preventative medicine and what to do in case of an emergency.

I've owned over 30 dogs in 15 years, training titled agility dogs and racing sled dogs. I've seen a lot of dogs during this time, my own and others, who benefited from good nutrition and good care. I've seen many diseases in dogs, from allergies to zinc responsive dermatosis and everything in between. I've also seen positive results with good care and nutrition. I've even rescued a dog who improved dramatically with good care and proper nutrition.

What You'll Find in This Book

This book is intended for both the first-time and experienced dog owner who wishes to learn more about health and nutrition. Some of the information within is quite complex, so if you feel the sudden urge to rush to the back of one of the chapters for "The Least You Need to Know," I'll understand completely. Know that the complex stuff is there in case you ever need it or wish to impress your friends at parties. (They did invite your dog, didn't they?)

This book is divided into five user-friendly parts:

Part 1, "Healthy Habits—Preventative Medicine," provides a basic overview of preventative care. These are things you can do to help prolong the health of your dog.

Part 2, "Trendy Pup: Trends in Dog Care," discusses the latest advances in vet care. It also discusses trends in health care such as holistic medicine and pet health insurance.

Part 3, "The Doctor Is In," provides an overview on maintaining your dog's health. You'll learn about genetic diseases and what constitutes an emergency. You find out why you really shouldn't breed your dog and what to do if your dog is pregnant. Lastly, you'll learn how to make your dog's senior years healthy and happy.

Part 4, "Dinnertime!" provides an overview of nutrition for dogs. You'll be surprised to learn that all dog food is not created equal. You'll also learn how to read a dog food label and what all those ingredients mean.

Part 5, "Nutrition Nuggets," gives an overview of special diets and whether homemade is really better than commercial. You'll learn how to select the right food according to your dog's age and activity level.

Extras

Check out the sidebars throughout the book. They're packed full of fun and informative facts.

Dog Treats
Great tips that will make your life easier.

No Biscuit!
Warnings about possible problems that might arise. Read these boxes carefully!

The Vet Is In
Interesting facts about nutrition or veterinary care.

Woofs
Definitions of terms used in this book.

Acknowledgments

Books don't appear out of thin air. This one certainly hasn't. I'm grateful to the help and guidance of the following people (in no particular order):

- Larry Bonham, my full-time husband and part-time editor. Couldn't do it without you.

- Jim Wingert, D.V.M., vet, tech editor, and co-author.

- Deb Eldredge, D.V.M., who patiently answered my questions and provided moral support. Thanks for the job lead. I appreciate it.

- Jessica Faust of Bookends, Inc. Thanks for the job!

- Mike Sanders, senior acquisitions editor, *The Complete Idiot's Guides*.

- Beth Adelman, technical editor and friend. Thank you for editing this book, plus thanks for the contacts to the AKC.

- Chuck Montera and the good folks at the American College of Veterinary Internal Medicine (ACVIM). Chuck arranged interviews with both Phil Bergman, D.V.M., and Karen Munana, D.V.M. Visit ACVIM's website at www.acvim.org.

- The good folks at the Animal Medical Center in NYC, including Shelby Thompson, Philip Bergman, D.V.M., and Susan Cohen, D.S.W., Visit the AMC website at www.amcny.org.

- Anna Bowie at the Denver Zoo and Nancy Irlbeck of Colorado State University.

- Mike Thomas, development editor, for his terrific job.

- Al Townshend, D.V.M. and Sonny King, D.V.M. for their information on sled dog nutrition and zinc responsive dermatosis.

🏠 Kim Thornton, fellow dog writer and brainstormer. She and I worked on different CIG books at the same time. Buy her book *The Complete Idiot's Guide to Beagles.*

A special thanks to Jessica John and Rocky, Tootie, and Makita; Dorothy Skeels and Ali and Benni; Peggi Pozder and Bucky and Buffy; Greg Olson and Casey Jo; Vicki Tucker and Sayde; Nancy Olson and Seven; Sandy and Tina Dugle of Dingo's Den Kennels, Alma Wirth, Jim Wingert and the staff at Broadview Animal Clinic for their patience with the photos.

A huge thanks to Albert and Betty Holowinski who made the photos possible.

Special Thanks to the Technical Reviewer

The Complete Idiot's Guide to Dog Health and Nutrition was reviewed by an expert who double-checked the accuracy of what you'll learn here, to help us ensure that this book gives you everything you need to know about feeding your dog right and keeping him healthy. Special thanks are extended to James M. Wingert, D.V.M.

Trademarks

All terms mentioned in this book that are known to be or are suspected of being trademarks or service marks have been appropriately capitalized. Alpha Books and Pearson Education, Inc., cannot attest to the accuracy of this information. Use of a term in this book should not be regarded as affecting the validity of any trademark or service mark.

Part 1 Healthy Habits— Preventative Medicine

Dogs are man's best friend, or so the saying goes. But who is a dog's best friend? You may be surprised to learn that it's you. As a dog owner, you're responsible for your dog's care and health. Vets can only do so much—if you're lucky, you and your dog will visit the vet only once a year for a checkup and shots.

Although genetics and luck play a certain role in whether your dog gets sick and how long he lives, most of his good health depends on you. Good nutrition, preventative care, and a watchful eye will go a long way in ensuring your dog's good health.

In Part 1, I discuss the basics of preventative care—how to find the right vet, how to examine and groom your dog, and how to give him medicine when he's sick. I discuss vaccinations—which ones are available and how to vaccinate your dog. I also cover how to spot a problem and how to know when it's time to go to the vet.

Chapter 1

To Your Health

In This Chapter

- 🏠 Learn why preventative care is so important for your dog
- 🏠 Discover how to find the best vet for both you and your dog
- 🏠 Identify what to expect at your puppy's first vet visit
- 🏠 Understand why nutrition is so crucial for your dog
- 🏠 Learn how poor nutrition can be devastating to a dog's health
- 🏠 Determine how to select the right diet for your dog

Proper health care and nutrition are important for your dog's long life. Just as people today have started taking better care of themselves through diet, preventative health care, and exercise, they are also looking to take better care of their dogs. Part of that care is through good nutrition and quality health care.

Finding a good vet is important for your dog's health. While there are many competent vets out there, you may have to do a little legwork to find the vet that's right for you and your dog.

Dog food isn't what it used to be. Thank goodness! Nowadays, pet food manufacturers spend millions of dollars studying, testing,

and formulating new diets for dogs. Dog food has evolved from generic brands to scientifically formulated, highly digestible food that is rich with Omega-3 fatty acids, glucosamine, sea kelp, and probiotics.

In this chapter, I discuss veterinarians, the types of practices and services they offer, and how to find a good one. I'll tell you a little about what to expect when you bring your dog in the first time. You'll also learn why nutrition is vitally important to dogs through-out their entire life, and how to select your dog's food.

The Importance of Preventative Care

A dog may be man's best friend, but from your dog's perspective, you are his best friend, especially when it comes to health and nutrition. You've no doubt heard the saying "An ounce of prevention is worth a pound of cure." The author could've been talking about veterinary care.

Advances in veterinary care have greatly increased pets' life spans and their quality of life. Dogs are able to live longer, more produc-tive lives, allowing them to be good companions and ready workers.

Two things affect your dog's quality of life: genetics and envi-ronment. While we still can't genetically engineer our next pet—although with research, that day will surely come—we can affect our dog's environment. Good nutrition, preventative health care, and a safe and happy environment will go a long way.

> **Dog Treats**
> Choose a vet who offers the services both you and your dog require. Flexible pay-ment plans and house calls are examples of two services you may need.

When we think of dog health care, it's natural that we think of a vet. Your vet is there to offer guid-ance in keeping your dog healthy, but ultimately, you are responsible for your dog's health. You are the first line of defense against sickness and poor health for your dog.

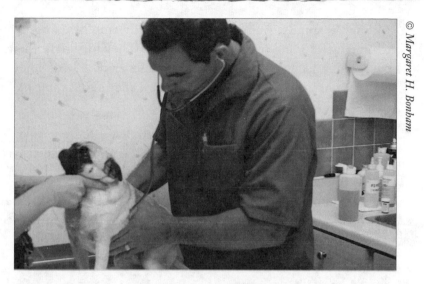

© Margaret H. Bonham

Choosing the right vet is important for your dog's health

Dog Doctors

Next to you, the veterinarian is your dog's best friend. When you look for a vet, he or she should be compatible with you. This may sound strange, but whether or not you get along with your vet will affect whether you're willing to follow his or her directions.

Not surprisingly, there are a multitude of dog doctors around. You may have one in the local strip mall next to the dry cleaners and fast-food takeout. But are these vets any good? And do they provide the kind of care that you're looking for?

Well, it depends. Nowadays, vets offer a variety of services, everything from emergency clinics, to specialists, to grooming. Some vets offer mobile clinics and true house calls. Others offer fast, convenient service and low prices; however, price shouldn't be your only consideration.

Different clinics include …

🏠 **Veterinary clinics.** Vet clinics may have as few as one or as many as five or more vets. These clinics have regular office hours and may or may not handle emergencies.

- **Animal hospitals.** Animal hospitals usually employ a large number of vets and may have specialists. They may have their own testing facilities, which smaller clinics can't afford. They may handle complex surgeries and emergencies that can't be treated anywhere else.

- **Emergency clinics.** These vet clinics are for emergencies only. They usually handle after-hours calls and tend to be expensive.

- **Low-cost clinics.** A relatively new type of vet clinic, the purpose behind most low-cost clinics is to provide routine services (vaccinations, heartworm tests, and spay/neuters) at a low price. These clinics make up for the lower price in volume. They generally don't have the facilities to handle emergencies or complex diagnoses.

- **Mobile clinics.** Usually limited in the services they provide, mobile clinics are often associated with an animal hospital or a veterinary clinic. These offer convenience to the pet owner. Mobile clinics usually charge more than a standard office visit due to the cost of fuel and may service a limited area.

© Margaret H. Bonham

You should have a good feeling about the veterinarian and the clinic before bringing your dog there.

How to Find the Best Dog Doc

So how do you find the right vet for your dog? It's quite simple: Ask your dog-owning friends whom they take their dogs to. The good vets don't need to advertise—usually all it takes is word-of-mouth.

If your friends don't give their vets glowing recommendations, perhaps you need to ask your dog's breeder, the animal shelter you adopted your dog from, or a local trainer. Even if your breeder doesn't live in your area, she might be able to ask local breeders whom they use for veterinarians. If that doesn't work, consider contacting the American Animal Hospital Association for a list of vets in your area.

Once you have a list of vets, call them and ask questions to help narrow down your choices. There are no right or wrong answers to the questions that follow, and some questions may be more important to you than others:

- What is the cost for vaccinations, office visits, and other routine services?
- What hours is your clinic open? Do you offer after-hours services?
- Do you handle emergencies or are you affiliated with a clinic that handles emergencies? Are the vets on-call and have an on-call pager?
- Do any of the vets specialize in a particular area such as allergies, neurology, or holistic treatments?
- Do you offer an on-site groomer or boarding?
- Do you offer a multi-pet discount?
- Do you take pet insurance?
- Do you make housecalls? Under what circumstances?
- How many dogs of my particular breed does the vet see?

The staff at the clinic should be courteous and willing to answer your questions.

Once you've narrowed down the vets to a few choices, schedule appointments to visit their facilities. Don't drop by unannounced—you may show up during a busy time when the staff won't have a chance to talk with you. When you do visit, ask for a tour. The clinic should be clean and the staff should be friendly and helpful. If you have a chance to talk with the vet, do so. Find out what the vet's training is and whether he or she is familiar with conditions common to your particular breed. If you're interested in alternative medicine, find out if the veterinarian uses alternative therapies or is strictly a conventional vet.

Dog Treats

If you're on a budget, perhaps a low-cost clinic will work for you. These clinics offer low prices on routine care, such as spays and neuters, vaccinations, and heartworm tests. But these clinics are seldom full-service facilities and are unable to handle emergencies or more complex procedures.

You should have a good feeling about the veterinarian and the clinic before bringing your dog there. Usually the final test is when you bring your dog for his first appointment. While some dogs won't get along with any vet, the vet should have a gentle and caring manner toward your dog.

Some vets offer boarding.

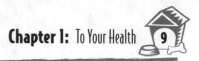
Meet the Vet—Your Dog's First Visit

Your dog's visit to the vet need not be traumatic. When you make an appointment, ask the receptionist if you should bring anything. Most vets would like any health records or vaccination records from previous vets. If your dog or puppy comes from a breeder or prior owner, they should have furnished your dog's vaccination record.

Some vets would like you to bring in a stool sample. If you bring it, be certain to bring it in a labeled plastic bag. (No one wants a nasty surprise!)

The Vet Is In

The average sled dog requires over 10,000 calories a day to run the Iditarod Trail Sled Dog Race. An adult human would have to consume 30,000 to 40,000 calories a day to burn the equivalent.

If this is a routine office visit, or your puppy's first visit, the veterinarian should give your dog a thorough exam. He should listen to your dog's heart and check him over for any problems. Most vets will ask what you're feeding your dog or puppy and make any recommendations. Your vet will most likely discuss proper dog or puppy health care and the benefits of spaying or neutering.

Now is the time to ask any questions concerning your dog's health. Don't feel silly asking questions—most vets have heard it all. If you don't understand something your vet says, ask!

Your vet will also discuss vaccinations with you. Depending on your vet's philosophy on vaccinations, you may be vaccinating your dog or puppy at this time. Follow your vet's advice with regard to vaccinations.

Why Nutrition Is Important to Dogs

"Garbage in, garbage out," the old saying goes. This saying applies especially well to dogs and dog food.

© Margaret H. Bonham

Nutrition plays a vital role throughout your dog's life.

What do you feed your dog? Most people simply rush out to the store for "Doggie Crunchies" and feed that. In most cases, they aren't doing anything wrong by feeding such products to their dogs. Most dog foods are *complete and balanced*, meaning that they're nutritionally complete for the average dog. But who has the average dog?

If you've picked up this book, you're probably not simply looking to maintain your dog, but to improve his health and performance. Perhaps your dog is a performance dog in flyball or agility. Maybe he hunts with you all day. Maybe he pulls a sled in races or works in search and rescue. Maybe he's a housepet; but whatever he is, he's your best friend and you want the best nutrition for him.

Good nutrition won't make a mediocre dog into a superstar, but it will help make him the best dog he can possibly be. Conversely, poor nutrition will ruin the best dog, regardless of how excellent his pedigree is or how wonderful his genetics.

Nutrition is vitally important to puppies, pregnant and lactating females, show dogs, and canine athletes. A good diet can help prevent certain diseases and health conditions. Good nutrition may help a dog live a longer, healthier life.

Nutrition plays an important role throughout your dog's life. When he is a puppy, he needs vital nutrients to grow into a healthy adult. When he is an adult, he needs good nutrition to keep his body functioning properly. Think of nutrition as building blocks—these blocks can be made of straw or brick, depending on what you feed your dog.

Your dog's food provides not only the building blocks for his body, but also the energy he requires. Your dog's body converts the calories in his food to energy to move and support his metabolism. Without this energy, your dog couldn't breathe, his heart couldn't pump blood, and his body couldn't regulate his temperature. He requires food that his body can convert into energy and use readily.

Woofs

Complete and balanced is a statement meaning that the dog food is nutritionally complete.

The Consequences of Bad Nutrition

When I speak of a malnourished dog, I'm referring to a dog that isn't getting enough nutrients. A dog can suffer from malnutrition and still get enough calories to maintain his weight. A fat dog can also suffer from malnutrition, even though he is getting more than enough calories in his diet.

Diet imbalances can cause significant consequences. For example, too much calcium can block absorption of key nutrients; too little calcium may cause severe bone loss, dangerous fractures, and even death. Excessive vitamin E is toxic, whereas too little may cause sudden death in working sled dogs. Poor nutrition can cause serious diseases and conditions. Luckily, many of these diseases are preventable—and sometimes even reversible—with a good diet.

I've seen firsthand what a poor diet does to a dog. One of my own rescue dogs, a German Shepherd Dog named Ranger, was obviously malnourished when I found him. Besides being thirty pounds

underweight (he weighed fifty pounds), he had apparently been fed a poor-quality diet. His legs were bowed, his coat flat and dull, and his teeth dirty. A new diet brought about miraculous changes: His teeth were clean and white and his coat improved substantially. His legs improved somewhat, but the damage was already done.

© Margaret H. Bonham

Premium commercial foods will provide good nutrition for a healthy dog.

In the 1970s, some commercial foods touted an all-meat diet. Unfortunately, dog owners were quick to feed their dogs only muscle meat, causing serious imbalances, most notably deficiencies in calcium and phosphorus. As a result, many dogs had to be euthanized.

How to Select Your Dog's Food

So, now you understand the importance of good nutrition and what bad nutrition can do to your dog. How do you find a good diet for your dog? Do you go to the local supermarket and pull a bag of Doggie Crunchies off the shelf? Do you cook an elaborate 10-course meal? Do you go to Chez Haute Boutique and buy the most expensive bag of kibble? Do you ask your vet?

In the "good old days" before kibble, people used to feed their dogs table scraps. We don't really know how long their dogs lived on average, but given that the average human life span was under forty years until the last two centuries, we can speculate that dogs didn't live all that long. Nowadays, we want our companions to live as long as possible, so it makes sense that we offer them the best nutrition we can.

 No Biscuit!

Feeding a dog table scraps as his main diet is unhealthy. Table scraps often contain high amounts of fat, salt, and fiber, and have very little nutritive value.

There are many fine commercial dog foods out there, but there's a lot of hype and misinformation, too. Some of this misinformation comes from folklore and anecdotal evidence—not hard fact. For example, the *Ethoxyquin* scare (see the following "The Vet Is In" sidebar) is a prime example of how public perception and rumors can hurt a product.

When you select your dog's food, base your choice not on what your friend feeds or what someone told you, but on its nutritional value and your dog's age and activity level. You should also select a food based on availability. You should be able to purchase the food from more than one source in case you run out or the distributor stops carrying it. Finally, your dog should like it. All the nutrition in the world does your dog no good if he won't eat it.

 The Vet Is In

Ethoxyquin is a preservative used in dog food. During the 1980s, Ethoxyquin was hailed as the "bad guy" in nutrition by the holistic crowd. It's been blamed for everything from allergies to cancer to miscarriages.

The truth is, there isn't one piece of evidence in any study that suggests ethoxyquin is bad. But misinformed dog owners began checking bags for the preservative and voted with their money. Many dog food manufacturers had to abandon the use of ethoxyquin in favor of less effective preservatives such as tocopherols.

Commercial vs. Homemade

In most cases, a premium commercial dog food is the right choice. However, there are situations where a premium dog food will not adequately fit your dog's special nutritional needs. Special needs include medical conditions and extreme performance requirements, such as those for sled dogs.

Most dog foods are formulated to the standards set forth by the American Association of Feed Control Officials (AAFCO). AAFCO guidelines offer the minimum requirements necessary for a dog's nutritional health. AAFCO provides guidelines for feeding puppy and adult dogs. Not all commercial dog foods are formulated to AAFCO guidelines. Look for a statement on the dog food that says it "meets or exceeds the guidelines set forth by the American Association of Feed Control Officials." If it does not, it cannot be considered complete.

Dog Treats

Select your dog food based on the following criteria:

- 🏠 Nutritional value
- 🏠 Your dog's age
- 🏠 Your dog's activity/fitness level
- 🏠 Availability
- 🏠 Palatability

Dog food companies spend millions of dollars on nutritional research each year and have the testing facilities to determine if the food has adequate amounts of nutrients. Most people who devise home-cooked diets don't have the ability to run an analysis to determine if what they are feeding meets or exceeds the guidelines set forth by AAFCO. If you must feed a homemade diet, consult a veterinary nutritionist.

Fad Diets

Every so often, fad diets crop up. These diets are typically touted as better for your dog than anything commercially produced. Proponents usually offer anecdotal evidence as proof that these diets are wonderful and do work.

The truth is that these diets can actually cause serious harm. Many aren't nutritionally complete. One, the "all-meat" diet, had serious nutritional imbalances that caused severe calcium deficiencies.

Vegetarian Diets

Some people believe that because they are vegetarians their dogs should be vegetarians, too. While dogs can and do subsist on vegetarian diets, they have evolved to be primarily carnivores. Dogs digest and use protein sources from animals more efficiently than from plant matter. Dogs also have difficulty digesting more complex carbohydrate sources.

No Biscuit!

Don't think that a dog food is nutritionally complete just because you bought it off the store shelf. Look for the statement that it meets or exceeds the guidelines set forth by AAFCO.

No Biscuit!

Never feed a dog an all-meat diet. All-meat diets are seriously deficient in key nutrients, most notably calcium.

Raw Diets

Raw diets, most notably the BARF (Bones and Raw Food) diet as made famous by Dr. Ian Billinghurst, are very popular among holistic pet owners. These diets are found in numerous books, but some commercial raw diets are also available.

Raw diets are a mixed blessing. Proponents claim that these diets are healthier for their dogs and cite their own experiences as proof. However, most users of raw diets are neither veterinarians nor nutritionists, and their claims are anecdotal at best.

When feeding a raw diet, you must take great care in handling the food because raw meat can harbor nasty bugs such as Salmonella and E. coli. Although touted as nutritionally balanced, a recent JAVMA (*Journal of the American Veterinary Medical Association*) article (March 2001) suggests that these diets are not. A nice compromise might be to supplement the diet with a balanced commercial food.

The Least You Need to Know

- 🐾 Know that the best way to find a good veterinarian in your area is word-of-mouth.

- 🐾 Remember that dogs require balanced nutrition for optimal health and performance.

- 🐾 Be cautious when feeding raw diets and homemade diets. Raw foods can harbor Salmonella and E. coli. Both diets may or may not be properly balanced.

- 🐾 Look for dog food formulated in accordance with AAFCO guidelines.

- 🐾 Avoid fad diets and diets that have no scientific basis.

- 🐾 Select your dog food based on the following criteria: nutritional value, dog's age, dog's activity/fitness level, availability, and palatability.

Preventative Care

In This Chapter

- 🏠 Understand the importance of vaccinations
- 🏠 Know why you should spay/neuter your dog
- 🏠 Learn how to examine your dog for health problems
- 🏠 Determine what kind of identification your dog needs
- 🏠 Learn how to give your dog medicines

Your dog will be healthier and happier when you take responsibility for his health. In this chapter, you'll learn about preventative care to keep your dog healthy and what signs to look for in a sick dog. You'll also learn why you should follow your vet's advice concerning vaccinations, how to give your dog medication without a struggle, and why tags, tattoos, and microchips are important aspects of your dog's safety and security.

Learning All About Vaccinations

Vaccinations help immunize your dog against deadly diseases such as rabies, distemper, and parvovirus. Some of these diseases, such as rabies and leptospirosis, which your dog can actually transmit to you and others, have a close to 100 percent mortality rate. Vaccinating your dog could save his life. For more information on these diseases, see "What Should You Vaccinate Your Dog Against?" later in this chapter.

Follow your vet's advice with regard to which vaccines your dog should receive and how often he should receive them.

Why Vaccinate?

Puppies receive maternal antibodies through their mother's *colostrum*. These maternal antibodies protect the puppy for several weeks. Sometime after the fifth week, these antibodies fade, leaving the puppy vulnerable to disease. That's where vaccinating your puppy comes in.

> **Woofs**
> **Colostrum** is the milk produced by the mother during the first 24 hours after her puppies are born.
> **Immune system response** is the production of antibodies against a disease.

> **No Biscuit!**
> Although allergic reactions to vaccines are uncommon, you should always watch your dog for a potential reaction. The most common reaction is swelling and puffiness in the face. A rare reaction is anaphylactic shock, where your dog has difficulty breathing and appears to be going into shock. If your dog shows any of these symptoms, call your vet immediately.

Vaccinations work by introducing into the body a small amount of the killed disease or modified version of the disease, which causes the body to fight against it. Because the vaccine can't cause the disease, the dog's body overwhelms the disease and continues to produce antibodies that will kill the actual disease if exposed to it. This response is called an *immune system response*.

Vets usually vaccinate puppies several times—it does no good to vaccinate a puppy before the maternal antibodies fade, because the antibodies will override the body's immune system response to the vaccination.

Unfortunately, we don't know when these antibodies go away—they vary from puppy to puppy—so vets try to vaccinate the puppy after the maternal antibodies go away but before the puppy becomes exposed to diseases. Distemper maternal antibodies usually fade between 10 and 12 weeks. Parvovirus maternal antibodies may not fade until 16 weeks.

Holistic Thoughts—What Are the Vaccination Controversies?

The current thinking is that vaccines work by producing an immune response in the dog each time a vet administers a vaccine. The question is: Are we overstressing our dogs' immune systems and causing *autoimmune disorders?*

Most holistic vets think we are overstressing our dogs' immune systems and recommend that we either don't vaccinate or change our current vaccination protocols to vaccinate less frequently. Many point out that dogs may keep their immunity to the disease for several years—not just for a year as previously thought.

Many veterinary colleges such as Colorado State University advise less frequent vaccinations. Yet, vaccine manufacturers still state all vaccines, except rabies, are only good for one year.

This is certainly a tough call. I tend to be conservative when it comes to vaccinations and opt to vaccinate once every year. A number of vets would agree with me, but vaccination technology is changing rapidly and the old methods may soon be obsolete. If you decide to not vaccinate yearly, you should consider running yearly tests to determine the *titers* on antibodies for both parvovirus and distemper in your dog.

Woofs

Autoimmune disorders are disorders wherein the dog's body produces an immune system response so often that it begins producing an immune system response for conditions that are not disease.

A **titer** is the level and strength of antibodies in a dog.

What about holistic vaccines, also called nosodes? Nosodes are not FDA approved for preventing any disease and there is no scientific evidence to show that they work. (See Chapter 6 for more information on nosodes.)

What Should You Vaccinate Your Dog Against?

As vaccination technology becomes more sophisticated, we may see more vaccines against different diseases. Recently, vaccine manufacturers have introduced Lyme and giardia vaccines. (See Chapter 9 for more information on Lyme and giardia.)

The Vet Is In

Canine Infectious Tracheobronchitis or kennel cough, is actually caused by a number of viruses and bacteria, including Bordetella bronchiseptica, canine parainfluenza, and canine adenovirus-2. In some ways it's like the common cold, because it has multiple agents—and it's just as difficult to prevent.

Does your dog need to be immunized against everything? Not necessarily. You should definitely vaccinate your dog against diseases such as rabies, parvovirus, and distemper, but the likelihood of exposure should dictate whether you need to vaccinate your dog against kennel cough, leptospirosis, giardia, and Lyme disease. Talk with your veterinarian about these vaccines and whether your dog is at high risk.

Your veterinarian has vaccines that will protect against the following diseases:

🐾 **Rabies.** This disease is caused by a virus and is nearly 100 percent fatal. There are two types of rabies: dumb (paralytic) and furious. Both types affect the central nervous system. In dumb rabies, the dog's throat becomes paralyzed, causing excessive salivation (drooling) and inability to swallow. Furious rabies is the classic mad dog form, where the dog becomes vicious and attacks anything. Furious rabies eventually progresses to the paralytic stage and death follows within a few days.

Rabies is contagious to humans and is transmitted through the dog's saliva—either through a bite or through wounds in the skin. The incubation period varies considerably, from three weeks to three months or more. Rabies is almost 100 percent fatal in all cases if contracted.

Canine Distemper (CDV). This disease is a virus that is nearly always fatal. Distemper starts with a yellow-gray discharge from nose and eyes, high temperature, dry cough, and lethargy. It may progress to appetite loss, diarrhea, and vomiting. Distemper may affect the intestinal tract or may attack the nervous system, causing seizures and convulsions. Some dogs may experience a hardening of the pads, hence the name hardpad disease. Canine Distemper is generally only contagious to canines, not humans.

Distemper is highly contagious among dogs and may be transmitted through the air, shoes, or clothing. Its incubation period is about 3 to 6 days. Treatment is generally supportive therapy.

Canine Adenovirus (CA$_2$). Canine Adenovirus 2 is a form of kennel cough. Dogs who contract kennel cough have a harsh, dry cough and may sound like they are gagging. Unless the dog is very old or young, kennel cough is more of a nuisance than a danger.

CA$_2$ is highly infectious and is transmitted through the air. The incubation period is between 5 and 10 days. Canine Adenovirus 2 is treated with cough suppressants from your vet and occasionally antibiotics for severe forms.

Infectious Canine Hepatitis (CA$_1$). Infectious Canine Hepatitis is a form of Adenovirus that causes fever, lethargy, jaundice (due to liver involvement), excessive thirst, vomiting, eye and nasal discharge, bloody diarrhea, hunched back, hemorrhage, and conjunctivitis. Infectious Canine Hepatitis may attack the kidneys, liver, eyes, and the lining of blood vessels. Both CA$_1$ and distemper may occur simultaneously. Infectious Canine Hepatitis is only contagious to canines, not humans.

It's contagious through an infected dog's urine, feces, and saliva. Its incubation period is between 4 and 9 days. Supportive therapy combined with antibiotics and blood transfusions (in severe cases) is used in treatment.

Canine Parainfluenza. Canine Parainfluenza is another form of kennel cough. Dogs who contract kennel cough have a harsh, dry cough and may sound like they are gagging. Unless the dog is very old or young, kennel cough is more of a nuisance than a danger.

It is highly infectious and is transmitted through the air. The incubation period is between 5 and 10 days. Canine Parainfluenza is treated with cough suppressants from your vet and occasionally antibiotics for severe forms.

Leptospirosis. This bacterial infection has symptoms that include high fever, frequent urination, brown substance on tongue, lack of appetite, renal failure, hunched back, bloody vomit and diarrhea, mild conjunctivitis, and depression. It is contagious to humans.

Dogs may contract leptospirosis from rats, infected water supplies, and other infected dogs. The incubation period is between 5 and 15 days. It is seldom fatal, with only a 10 percent mortality rate. Newer versions of this disease have a higher death rate. Treatment consists of antibiotics and supportive therapy. Leptospirosis can be a serious disease in humans, so contact your doctor if your dog is diagnosed with it.

Canine Parvovirus. This nasty virus appeared in 1978. It's characterized by severe, bloody diarrhea, vomiting, dehydration, high fever, and depression. Canine Parvovirus is only contagious to canines, not humans.

It is highly infectious and is transmitted through fecal matter. The virus can live up to one year in the soil and can be carried on shoes or paws. It has a 7- to 10-day incubation period and a 50 percent mortality rate. Puppies under one year of age are at greater risk in contracting parvovirus. Treatment consists of supportive therapy, treating the diarrhea, vomiting, and dehydration.

Canine Coronavirus. A less deadly virus than parvovirus, coronavirus looks a lot like a milder form of parvovirus. Indeed, both parvovirus and coronavirus may infect a dog simultaneously. Canine Coronavirus is only contagious to canines, not humans.

Coronavirus is transmitted through fecal matter. It has a 24- to 36-hour incubation period. Treatment consists of supportive therapy, treating the diarrhea, vomiting, and dehydration.

Bordetella bronchiseptica. Bordetella bronchiseptica is a form of kennel cough. Dogs who contract kennel cough have a harsh, dry cough and may sound like they are gagging. Unless the dog is very old or young, kennel cough is more of a nuisance than a danger.

It is highly infectious and is transmitted through the air. The incubation period is between 5 and 10 days. Bordetella bronchiseptica is treated with cough suppressants from your vet and occasionally antibiotics for severe forms.

Lyme (Borellosis). Lyme disease is a tick-borne disease that appeared in Lyme, Connecticut, in 1975. Lyme is fairly common along the East Coast and Upper Midwest in the United States, and continues to spread. Lyme's symptoms—fever, lameness, loss of appetite, and fatigue—are similar to other diseases and can make the disease difficult to diagnose.

Lyme is transmitted through deer ticks. The primary hosts are deer and mice. Lyme disease is treatable in the early stages through antibiotics.

Giardia. Giardia is a microscopic organism that lives in streams. Carried by beavers and other wildlife, as well as domesticated animals, giardia was confined to the Rocky Mountains, but may be found in any untreated water. Giardia causes severe diarrhea, vomiting, and weight loss.

Dog Treats

If you aren't sure what vaccinations are appropriate for your dog, ask your vet. Your vet will have a better understanding as to what diseases are common in your area.

Giardia is treated with metronidazole (Flagyl, obtained through your vet or doctor) or similar medication in both dogs and humans. Because giardia is a tough parasite, there may be a need for subsequent treatments.

Vaccinating Your Dog Yourself

You may be surprised to learn that in many states you can purchase vaccines and vaccinate your dog yourself. There are many positives and negatives associated with vaccinating your dog. The positive is obvious. If you have multiple dogs, you can save a lot of money. Vaccines typically cost $2 to $10 a vaccine, depending on the vaccine and the area. This is good for kennel owners and for pet owners who can't afford the cost of vaccinations. The downsides of vaccinating your dogs however, may outweigh the savings:

- You don't know how the vaccines were handled prior to your receiving them. While vaccines can sometimes tolerate a day of room temperature, I wouldn't trust the viability of the vaccine if it has reached room temperature. Most pet supply stores will overnight vaccine shipments at an extra charge.

- Sometimes over-the-counter vaccines are old-style vaccines and aren't the best available. Your vet should keep up on the latest vaccines and know which are the best for your dog.

- You can cause serious problems by administering a vaccination incorrectly. Some vaccines are made for subcutaneous, intermuscular, or intranasal injection only. You can make your dog sick, invalidate the vaccination, or even kill your dog by injecting him incorrectly.

🏠 Your dog could have an anaphylactic reaction to the vaccine. These reactions are rare, but there is always that potential. Some reactions are mild—others are serious and could result in death.

🏠 Most vaccines come in 10-dose or 25-dose packs. Because of FDA regulations, these vaccinations can't be sold out of package. You must either purchase the vaccines with other dog owners or be able to use the vaccines within a year or less.

🏠 Syringe and needle disposal are tricky. You can't simply toss the syringe and needle out because this is a biohazard.

🏠 Vaccination schedules change. The vaccination schedule for dogs and puppies varies, depending on need and the risk of exposure to your dog. Your vet has a good idea what your dog should be vaccinated against.

🏠 In some states it is illegal for you to vaccinate your dog for rabies or even to vaccinate your dog at all.

🏠 You may have trouble proving that you vaccinated your dog if you want to board him or if he bites someone.

🏠 Vets often catch health problems through routine examinations performed during vaccinations.

Clearly, there are downsides to vaccinating your dog yourself. But if you own a kennel of dogs or have a lot of dogs to vaccinate at once, the cost savings may be worth considering.

> **Dog Treats**
> There are low-cost alternatives to vaccinating your dog yourself or spending lots of money. Some vets, breed clubs, shelters, and discount vet clinics offer low-cost vaccination clinics. Some vets will match the price of these lower-cost clinics to retain your business.

Vaccinating your dog is relatively simple, but it's best to have someone who has done it before show you how to do it. Subcutaneous vaccinations are given under the skin—usually just under the folds of skin where the back of the neck and the shoulders meet.

Inter-muscular vaccinations are usually given in the meaty part of the hip and straight into the muscle. Mix the vaccine according to directions and remove as much of the air as possible from the syringe. If giving the vaccine by inter-muscular or subcutaneous injection, use rubbing alcohol on the injection sight, insert the needle and pull back to make certain you haven't hit a blood vessel. (If you've hit a blood vessel, blood will show in the syringe. Remove the needle and try again.) Avoid injecting a nerve—this will cause the dog to limp. After you inject the vaccine, watch for allergic reactions.

No Biscuit!

Seek immediate veterinary attention if your dog shows any of the following symptoms after a vaccination:

- 🏠 Difficulty breathing or cessation of breathing
- 🏠 Choking
- 🏠 Swelling in the face or around the injection site
- 🏠 Sleepiness or lethargy
- 🏠 Hives or rash
- 🏠 Rapid breathing, nervousness
- 🏠 Unconsciousness

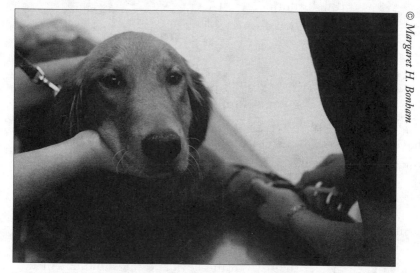

© Margaret H. Bonham

Despite this dog's pathetic look, the heartworm test only requires a little bit of blood. Follow your vet's advice concerning heartworm.

Heartworm Preventative

Your vet may wish to start your dog on heartworm preventative, depending on whether you're in a heartworm area. Heartworm is a very nasty internal parasite that can kill your dog. You should have your dog tested for heartworm once a year and put on preventative.

Most veterinarians now prescribe monthly heartworm preventatives, although there are still a few daily preventatives available. Do not use the daily preventatives, as they are less effective than the monthly preventatives if administered incorrectly.

There are several types of heartworm preventative available, including some that also help control other worms. These include:

- **Heartgard (Ivermectin).** This is the oldest form of monthly heartworm preventative. The Heartgard Plus brand includes pyrantel pamoate for control of roundworms and hookworms. Note that some dogs are sensitive to Ivermectin, but this sensitivity is rare. The most common sensitive dogs are Collies and Shetland Sheepdogs, but other breeds and mixed breeds can be affected.

- **Interceptor (Milbemycin) and Sentinel (Milbemycin and Lufenuron).** Interceptor controls heartworms as well as hookworms, roundworms, and whipworms in a monthly preventative. Sentinel also controls fleas.

- **Revolution (Selamectin).** A topical application, Revolution works as a monthly heartworm and flea preventative.

- **Proheart 6 (Moxidectin).** A six-month preventative, Proheart 6 is given as an injection and can only be administered by your vet.

The Vet Is In
Your dog will be healthier and happier if he is spayed or neutered before one year. Spaying and neutering reduces or eliminates a number of potential health risks such as ovarian cancer, mammary tumors, and pyometra in females and testicular cancer and anal tumors in males.

Understanding the Great Spay/Neuter Debate

Most dog owners have heard that they should spay or neuter their dogs. Still, many don't comply. There are numerous reasons to spay and neuter, including health benefits, but many owners are still under the misconception that spaying and neutering will somehow make their dog less valuable.

This reluctance seems to be particularly true with purebred owners. Just because you paid a lot of money for your purebred doesn't mean that your purebred should be bred. Quite the contrary! Most purebreds should *not* be bred. Most purebreds are not of breeding quality and will pass on undesirable traits to their offspring, producing substandard dogs and adding to the already burgeoning pet overpopulation.

Unless your dog competes professionally in dog shows, there is really no reason to keep an intact dog.

But let's talk about some of the common myths and misconceptions surrounding spaying and neutering:

- 🏠 **My dog will get fat and lazy.** Overeating and lack of exercise cause your dog to get fat and lazy. However, some dogs do become more interested in food after neutering and spaying and you may have to cut back his rations a bit.

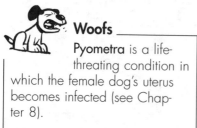

Woofs

Pyometra is a life-threatening condition in which the female dog's uterus becomes infected (see Chapter 8).

- 🏠 **It's healthier for a female to have a litter of puppies.** Actually, it's not. If you spay a female while young, you decrease the risk of mammary tumors and eliminate a life-threatening disease called *pyometra.*

🏠 **My dog will miss sex.** The truth is that sex is a purely instinctual drive in a dog and that dogs don't get any pleasure or enjoyment from it. Breeding isn't pleasurable—it's instinctual, and if you've ever seen two dogs mate, you know it can also be downright painful.

🏠 **My female should have a litter of puppies to enhance her maternal instincts.** Some females do go through behavior changes, but not necessarily for the better. Females that don't have puppies don't think about having puppies, nor do they miss them.

🏠 **My male dog will be less aggressive and less protective.** If you're looking for an aggressive, protective dog, then you should also look at purchasing good liability insurance. Aggressiveness is not appropriate for a pet *under any circumstances*. You can be sued or even jailed for owning a vicious dog. Protectiveness varies according to the individual dog, training, and the bond between the owner and dog. Spaying or neutering will help your dog focus on you and not instinctive drives.

If you want a protection dog, neutered dogs do just as well as intact dogs in training. They may be more reliable, too, because they aren't combating hormones.

No Biscuit!
Dogs that are intact are prone to more behavior and health problems than their neutered counterparts.

🏠 **My dog won't act male.** Actually, he will. It's a little-known fact that neutered males will try to mate with females in season—and will succeed, except for one thing—they won't reproduce. Neutered males may take a little extra time to lift their legs, but they eventually do. Also, neutering actually makes a young dog bigger because the growth plates close later.

Why You Should Spay/Neuter Your Dog

Most dog owners are aware of the pet overpopulation. Every year, approximately five million pets show up in shelters, about a quarter of them purebred dogs. You may not be aware though, that a good portion of mixed breeds are actually crossbreeds—that is, dogs that are one half purebred and half another.

Many purebred owners fail to spay or neuter their dogs because they are "valuable" purebreds. Then, one little accident and the dog has puppies. Not surprisingly, they're not purebred, so the owners get rid of them.

While you may find homes for these puppies, it decreases the likelihood for other mixed breeds finding potential homes. And how many homes actually keep a dog for life? Did you screen potential owners thoroughly? The truth is, you've just added to the pet overpopulation.

Dog Treats

If you have a multi-dog household, you may see less aggression between them if all the dogs are spayed and neutered. I've seen a remarkable turnaround in my dogs—including females.

Dog Treats

The best time to examine your dog for abnormalities such as bumps and lumps is while grooming him.

Health and Behavior Benefits

There are other reasons for spaying and neutering your dog, namely health and behavior. You may be surprised to learn that spaying and neutering helps improve your dog's temperament. Dogs that are spayed or neutered tend to focus more on you than on the mating drive. With a spayed female, there's no estrus, meaning that you don't have to cloister her away for a month twice a year. With males, you're not fighting the sometimes overpowering drive to look for females in season.

Neutered males are less likely to develop anal tumors. Neutering eliminates testicular cancer as well. Spayed females are less likely to develop mammary tumors if spayed before two years of age and won't develop ovarian and uterine cancers. They also won't develop pyometra.

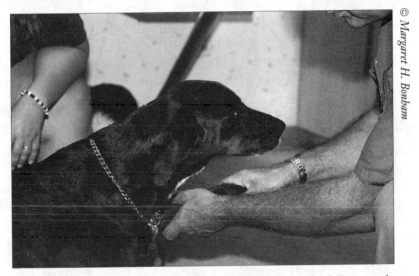

While examining your dog, you should check your dog's legs for full range of motion.

Giving Your Dog a Health Exam

You should make it a weekly ritual to examine your dog, preferably while grooming him. Start with your dog's head and work your way back. Look for abnormalities such as bumps and lumps. If you feel what might be a lump, check the other side of your dog in the same place; if there's one there, too, you can safely discount the lumps as normal.

Be sure to check the following as part of your dog's weekly health exam:

🏠 **Eyes.** Your dog's eyes should be clear and bright without excessive or pus-like discharge. There should be no redness or tearing.

🐾 **Nose.** Your dog's nose should be cool to touch and moist. A hot and dry nose may indicate fever. There should be no discharge or blood.

🐾 **Ears.** Your dog's ears should be clean and sweet-smelling. Any foul odor or excessive buildup of wax indicates a potential ear problem.

🐾 **Mouth.** Your dog's teeth should be white and clean, without tartar buildup. Your dog's breath should not be foul-smelling—if it is, it may suggest tooth or gum problems. Are the gums a healthy pink or are they red?

🐾 **Legs.** Feel down your dog's legs to check for any lumps or bumps. Inspect the footpads for cuts and foreign objects such as foxtails. Look at the toenails—they shouldn't be red or broken. If you find an unusual bump, check the other side. If the bump is unilateral (it's only on one side) then it might be a tumor. Check the legs for full range of motion, moving them slowly and gently in full range. There should be no clicks or pops.

🐾 **Skin and fur.** Determine if there are any sores, bald patches, or redness to the skin. Is the skin dry or flaky? Are there dark grains through the fur that turn red when wet? (These are flea feces.)

🐾 **Tail.** Is the tail healthy-looking or hanging limp? Has your dog been chewing on it?

🐾 **Sexual organs.** Is there discharge from the vagina or penis? (Note that in intact female dogs, discharge is normal during estrus.)

No Biscuit!

Your dog should always have two forms of ID on him: his tags and either a tattoo or microchip. Never allow your dog out of the house without a collar and tags.

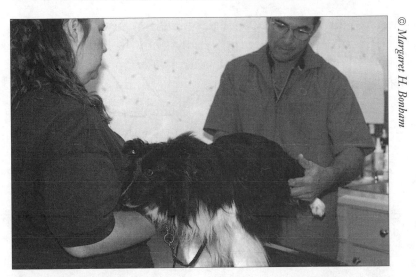

© Margaret H. Bonham

There should be no clicks or pops as you move your dog's leg slowly through normal range of motion.

ID, Please—Tags, Microchips, and Tattoos

Although you might not think of identification as a health topic, it is vital for your dog's safety and security that he has two forms of ID on him at all times. First, he should have tags on his collar as an easy means of identification. Second, I recommend one of two more permanent methods of identification: microchips and tattoos. I'll cover all three in this section.

Tags

Tags are a cheap form of identification. Most tags cost between $4 and $8, although if you have to have the 24-carat gold-plated tags or the tags with a blessing from St. Francis of Assisi, they may be between $10 and $20. They're relatively easy to obtain, too. Your vet probably has mail-in forms at his office, but you can purchase them through pet supply mail-order catalogues, online (I've actually gotten free tags from some Internet suppliers), or even from large pet supply stores. Many pet supply stores now have tag-engraving machines. For $4 to $8, you have a tag you can put on your dog's collar right there in the store—no waiting for the mail.

Given how easy and cheap it is to put a tag on your dog's collar, there is absolutely no reason that your dog should be without tags. Make two tags, and keep one as a spare. Tags can fall off, and every day lost dogs turn up at shelters with collars, but without tags. Most owners forget or fail to put tags on their pets. Don't be one of them!

> **Dog Treats**
>
> Three ID registries for dogs are the National Dog Registry (NDR), Tattoo-A-Pet, and Home Again. (See Appendix B.)

Permanent Forms of ID—Tattoos and Microchips

What if your dog loses his tag or collar? What if someone finds your dog and decides to keep him? Or worse yet, suppose someone *steals* your dog? What then? A permanent form of ID on your dog, either a Tattoo or Microchip, is the answer to these questions.

You can get tattoos done at a vet clinic, through a breed club, or from a groomer. Both NDR and Tattoo-A-Pet can refer you to tattooists in your area. Vets, and sometimes animal shelters, provide microchips. Talk with your vet about both forms of permanent ID.

Here's the lowdown on these two forms of permanent identification:

🏠 **Tattoos are a permanent form of ID.** There are two locations on a dog's body where tattoos are put: inside the ears or on the inside thigh. Inside the ears is a poor choice—dog thieves will often lop off an ear to remove the identification.

Tattoos are generally painless, but they are noisy and most dogs hate having it done. They are less expensive than microchips. You must choose a unique number for your dog—most people choose their Social Security number or American Kennel Club (AKC) number. However, those numbers must be registered with an ID registry.

🏠 **Microchips are about the size of a grain of rice.** They are encased in plastic, and are activated only when a scanner is passed over them. You must have a vet perform the procedure, which takes only a few seconds and causes very little discomfort. The microchip is implanted between the shoulder blades. When the scanner is passed over it, it reads the microchip in the same way a grocery scanner reads the bar code on a product. If someone finds your dog, they can have a vet scan for the microchip. Then the vet contacts the registry to look up the dog in the database to find the owner.

There are pluses and minuses to both forms of identification. First, most people don't know to check for either tattoos or microchips. Most people, even if they find the tattoo, don't know the registries out there. With microchips, even if the person did know to check for microchips, scanners aren't cheap and many scanners don't work with all possible microchips. There is no standard for microchips at this time, although the American Kennel Club (AKC) has introduced the Home Again chip and registration.

Not all shelters have scanners for microchips, although Home Again and other microchip manufacturers have offered microchip scanners at free or low cost to shelters.

How much do tattoos and microchips cost? You're paying for either the tattoo or microchip, plus the registration. Some breed clubs offer tattoo clinics for $10 to $20 a dog plus the registration fee. The lowest cost I've seen for a microchip clinic is $25 a dog plus registration fee. Expect to pay anywhere from $30 to $80 for a tattoo and registration and $50 to $125 for a microchip and registration.

Giving Your Dog Medications

Occasionally, your vet may ask you to administer medications to your dog. The most frequent are pills, but occasionally you may have to give liquids.

It helps if your dog is comfortable with you touching his mouth. Start at an early age to get him used to you touching his mouth. (Brushing his teeth is an ideal time for this.) Once your dog is used to you touching his mouth, giving medications is less stressful.

Pill Popping

People seem to have a hard time giving their pets pills. The truth is, practice makes perfect. Most dogs will swallow a pill readily if you open their mouths, pop the pill into the back of their mouths, and close their jaws with their head tilted upward. Stroking the underside of the throat helps too. Some pet owners use a little device called a pet piller. It does the same thing, only a little more accurately, so if your aim to the back of the throat is lousy, try one of these.

If you can't get the hang of either method, try peanut butter. Most dogs love peanut butter; it sticks to the roof of their mouth—which provides hours of entertainment for the owner—and gets the pill down without a fuss. An alternative is to hide the pill in a piece of hotdog (do they even taste it?) or some other treat. If the pill can be ground up (some can't—check with your vet), try mixing it with one of his meals.

Liquid Medications

Liquid medications are fairly easy to administer. Ask your vet for an oral syringe with the amount marked on the syringe in permanent marker. Fill the syringe and then pull your dog's lower lip out, near where it joins the upper lip, to form a pouch. Squirt the medication gently into the pouch, release it, and tilt your dog's head back. He will swallow automatically.

Eye Ointment

Another medicine dog owners may need to administer is eye ointment. Eye ointment usually comes in tubes. Depending on how big your dog is, you may need two people to administer it. Have someone hold your dog's head gently. Pull down the lower eyelid and expose the eyelid's underside. Squeeze the prescribed amount of ointment in the eyelid's underside and release. The dog will blink, coating the eye. Do the same for the other eye, if required.

The Least You Need to Know

- When it comes to vaccinating your dog, your vet knows best.
- Your dog will be healthier and better behaved if he or she is neutered or spayed.
- Spaying or neutering keeps your dog from contributing to the pet overpopulation.
- You need to examine your dog at least once a week for signs of illness and abnormalities.
- Your dog should have two forms of ID—tags and a permanent form of ID, such as a microchip or tattoo.
- It is easy to give medications to your dog if you know how. Try mixing the medication with his food or hiding it in a treat if you have trouble.

3

Beauty Parlor:
Grooming Your Dog

In This Chapter

🏠 Hiring a groomer versus doing it yourself

🏠 Finding a reputable groomer

🏠 Grooming your dog, from teeth to toenails

Part of your dog's health relies on good grooming. Depending on his breed and type of coat, your dog may be easy to groom or nearly impossible. Have no fear! There are groomers who will groom your dog, whether his coat is wash-and-wear or requires clipping and fussing over.

In this chapter, you'll learn about the importance of grooming your dog as part of his preventative care regimen. You'll learn the basics of brushing, combing, and bathing as well as cleaning your dog's ears, brushing his teeth, and clipping his toenails.

The Importance of Grooming

Grooming your dog is important for the health of his coat and skin. Not to mention that your dog will be less stinky! But whether you should groom your dog or have someone else groom him is up to you. If you have the time and are willing to groom your own dog, then good for you! But be honest with yourself. Nowadays, people have less time to do the things they *want* to do—let alone the things they *don't* want to do. Don't let your dog's health suffer because you don't have time to groom him.

 Dog Treats

Grooming need not be a hassle. Start training your dog when he is a puppy to accept grooming. Some dogs, believe it or not, grow to like grooming.

Do It Yourself or Hire Someone?

Grooming a dog *can* be a daunting task, especially if you work or if your dog has a high-maintenance coat. If you're a busy person, paying for a groomer every other week or every month might be worthwhile, especially if you can't take the time to do routine grooming. If your dog has a long or double coat, requires extra clipping and styling, or is especially dirty or matted, the groomer will charge you more than he would a less dirty dog or one with less hair.

No Biscuit!

Owners of seizure-prone dogs should be especially careful when bringing their dogs to the groomer. Be certain that the groomer doesn't use sedatives or tranquilizers. Medications such as Acepromazine (a common veterinary sedative) can cause an epileptic dog to go into seizures.

A groomer will do a professional job on your dog, but if your dog is difficult to work with or aggressive, the groomer may have to tranquilize him. Because some breeds and some dogs are particularly sensitive to tranquilizers, you should probably avoid using groomers who tranquilize.

How to Find a Reputable Groomer

Ask other dog owners which groomers they use. Often, a good recommendation is worth checking into. If you do not know anyone who uses a groomer, ask your vet. Your vet can usually recommend a groomer or may even have one onsite.

Once you have selected a particular groomer you're interested in, contact the groomer and ask what kinds of services he or she performs. Some groomers will do nails and express anal glands, for example. Ask how long the groomer has been in business and what types of training and certifications he or she has. While many good groomers do not have certifications, you will help weed out those who are not qualified to work on dogs. Ask the groomer how many clients he or she sees monthly. Ask how many dogs are dogs of your breed. Last, ask for references.

Visit the grooming shop and look around. If they're busy, you may see hair and water on the floor, but otherwise the grooming area should be clean and well organized. Dogs in crate dryers should be watched and checked frequently—a dog can seriously overheat and die if left unattended in a crate dryer.

Make certain that unless your dog is aggressive or unless the job is extreme, the groomers use no medications to tranquilize dogs. Some groomers will use muzzles in the case of aggressive or hard to handle dogs. If your dog is old or has joint problems, find out what the groomer will do to make the experience more comfortable.

 Dog Treats ____

If your friends or vet can't recommend a groomer, contact the National Dog Groomers Association of America at 412-962-2711 and ask for members in your area.

Woofs ____

A single coat is a coat that is similar to human hair—that is, it has no undercoat.

A double coat is a coat with an undercoat that adds extra insulation.

Wash-and-Wear—Grooming Your Dog Yourself

You should groom your dog at least once a week. This includes brushing and combing his coat, clipping his toenails, and brushing his teeth. Depending on your dog's coat, you may also wish to clip him.

Always comb out your dog before bathing him. Dog shampoos are pH balanced, so you can bathe your dog as often as you like without stripping the coat of its oils.

Coat of Many Colors

How often you groom your dog depends on his coat and whether he is shedding or dirty. If your dog has a *single coat*, like a poodle or some terriers, he will need clipping and styling. If your dog has a *double coat*, he may need extra grooming to remove his undercoat when he sheds.

© *Margaret H. Bonham*

Brush your dog's hair against the lay of the coat and then brush it back.

Both types of coats need brushing at least once a week. Depending on the breed and type of coat, you may have to brush and comb your dog every day. Dogs such as Soft Coated Wheaten Terriers and Keeshonden have high-maintenance coats, whereas short-coated breeds such as Greyhounds and Labradors have very low-maintenance coats. Check a breed manual for your particular breed and coat care.

All dogs with undercoats shed. Northern breeds such as Alaskan Malamutes, Siberian Huskies, Samoyeds, and similar breeds shed profusely twice a year. Other breeds may shed only once a year or may shed year-round.

Dog Treats

A warm bath will often loosen the fur on a dog in the middle of shedding or "blowing" his coat.

Tools of the Trade

Naturally, you'll need some standard supplies for grooming your dog. These include the basic brushes and combs, but also include what might seem like extravagance: items such as a dog blow dryer and grooming table. These items, however, will make your job much easier. Grooming tables will help save your back, and dog blow dryers won't burn your dog's skin.

Here's a complete list of tools you need:

- Slicker brush
- Long-tooth comb
- Flea comb
- Zoom Groom™ or Curry Brush (short coat)
- Undercoat rake (double coat)
- Nail clippers or nail grinder

- Styptic powder

- Shears (single coat)

- Thinning shears (single coat)

- Electric clipper (single coat)

- Shampoo formulated for dogs

- Creme rinse formulated for dogs

- Grooming table with noose

- Blow dryer for dogs—not a blow dryer for humans, they are too hot

- Mat splitter or mat rake (double coat)

- Toothpaste and toothbrush for dogs (do not use toothpaste for humans)

> **Dog Treats**
>
> A recent phenomenon is do-it-yourself dog washes. For a few bucks, you can bring your dog into a dog-wash facility and use its soap, towels, and grooming tools. Many have grooming tables as well as dog-wash tubs.

Brushing and Combing

Start by brushing the hair and untangling any mats. (Use a mat splitter or a detangler solution.) Next, brush your dog's hair against the lay of the hair. This helps stimulate oils in the coat. Then brush the dog's hair back, in the direction of growth.

Giving Baths

Although it's tempting, you should never bathe a dog without first brushing him out. Some breeds are prone to tangles and their hair will mat worse if you bathe them first. Instead, brush your dog out and then bathe him with a good pH balanced shampoo for dogs.

(Do not use shampoo for humans.) Follow it with a creme rinse made for dogs and rinse thoroughly.

Some dogs hate baths. Sometimes this is because the owner isn't careful to keep the soap out of the dog's eyes and ears. You may want to consider putting a small piece of cotton in each ear so that the water doesn't get in. Be certain that the water is tepid to the touch (no hot showers!). Rinse your dog really well because the soap and creme rinse will attract dirt. Be careful to not get any soap in your dog's eyes.

Use a dog blow dryer to dry your dog. Don't use a human hair dryer, as these are too hot and will burn your dog's skin and scorch his fur. Use towels to get rid of the excess water and then blow his fur dry.

Clipping

Clipping and scissoring is best left to the professionals the first few times. Have someone familiar with clipping and styling give you some pointers on how your breed should look. (The groomer may show you how to maintain a certain pet cut between visits.) Practice does make perfect and the good news is that the hair does grow out. Just be very careful of ears and skin so that you don't nick or cut them. Never use scissors to clip or cut out mats. You can seriously cut your dog (see the accompanying "No Biscuit!" sidebar).

 **No Biscuit!**

Never clip or cut mats out of your dog's fur. No matter how careful, people end up cutting their dog's skin, which requires a trip to the emergency animal hospital for sutures. If your dog is badly matted, have a professional groomer handle the mats.

Have someone who knows how to use clippers show you how to properly use them. Most groomers will show you how to maintain your dog's coat between professional clippings.

Pearly Whites—Keeping the Doggie Dentist at Bay

Doggie dentistry may sound humorous, but it's serious business. Infected teeth can cause severe health problems, including heart problems, in your dog. Teeth cleaning requires anesthesia and its associated risks—not to mention expense!

The Vet Is In

Adult dog teeth are actually twice the size of what you see. The long roots help give dogs the biting power necessary for carnivores to chew meat and bone.

Many vets recommend brushing your dog's teeth every day with toothpaste specially formulated for dogs. Quite honestly, most dog owners don't have the time or patience to do that, so I recommend brushing your dog's teeth once a week to reduce plaque which leads to tartar. If your dog has good teeth (and healthy teeth and gums largely depend on genetics and diet), you might be able to get away with brushing his teeth less often, but that's inadvisable.

Brushing Your Dog's Teeth

Naturally, your dog is first going to have to become used to you touching his mouth. To get him used to it, start by holding your dog's head gently and flipping up his lip and touching his teeth and gums. Do this gently and praise him. Practice this often, so he becomes used to you touching his mouth.

After he becomes used to you handling his mouth, get a soft washcloth and wet a corner of it. Now, with your finger, gently massage your dog's gums with the tip of the washcloth.

The next step is to get a toothbrush designed for dogs. Use toothpaste formulated for pets. (Never use human toothpaste, as it is poisonous to dogs.) Most are chicken- or malt-flavored, so the taste is appealing. Your dog doesn't have to rinse and spit!

 No Biscuit!
Never use human toothpaste to brush your dog's teeth. The fluoride in the toothpaste is poisonous to pets. Use toothpaste made for pets.

Recognizing a Tooth or Gum Problem

Hopefully, your dog will go through life without a tooth or gum problem. If you feed him a nutritious diet and give him plenty of chewing toys, you minimize the need for teeth cleaning. However, your dog may still have a tooth or gum problem. Learn to recognize potential warning signs, and visit the vet when they arise:

- Loss of appetite
- Sudden, unexpected chewing on inappropriate items
- Sudden change in chewing habits or lack of chewing

- Bad breath
- Nasal discharge
- Red, swollen gums
- Lump above or below a particular tooth

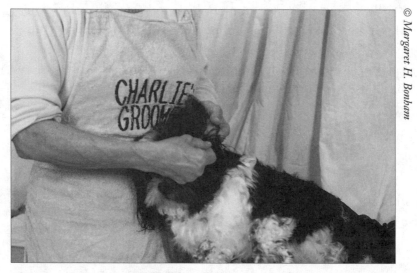

© Margaret H. Bonham

When you clean your dog's ears, be certain to remove all excess cleaner to prevent infection.

Do You Hear What I Hear?

Some dogs develop ear problems frequently; others never seem to have a problem. Breeds that seem to have a predisposition for ear infections and injuries tend to be sporting dogs and hounds due to their dropped ears. Dropped ears make an ideal place for bacteria to grow and mites to hide.

Regardless of the breed, you should keep your dog's ears clean. Your dog's ears should be clean and sweet-smelling. If there is an odor, your dog may have an infection.

Cleaning Your Dog's Ears

Use a mild otic solution for dogs. Squeeze some into your dog's ears and then gently massage the outside of the ear canal. Now, take sterile gauze or sponges and gently wipe out the excess. Never leave any excess in the ear or it can cause ear infections. Clean your dog's ears once a week.

Don't use insecticides or mite treatments, as this can cause irritation. If you suspect ear mites, see your vet for the appropriate treatment.

Recognizing an Ear Problem

These are the signs of potential ear problems, which suggest that it's time to visit the vet:

- Your dog scratches at, paws, or shakes his head.
- There is a foul-smelling odor coming from his ears.
- Ears have an excessive waxy buildup.
- Ears are crusty or red.
- You see a red or black waxy buildup.

Tap Dancing—Clipping Your Dog's Toenails

Dogs hate having their toenails clipped. Most would rather live with a cat than have you come near them with that evil "clippy thing." You can avoid, or at least minimize, the hassle if you get your dog used to having his toenails clipped when he is a puppy.

Start by getting your puppy used to you handling his feet. Touch, pick up, and hold each foot gently. For the first few times, it may be no longer than a few seconds. Gradually increase the time you hold your puppy's feet.

Clip your dog's nails once a week to keep them short and healthy. Long nails may break and cause pain.

Be sure you clip only the tips of the nail. If you clip too far up the nail, you risk cutting into the *quick*. The quick is that part of a dog's nail that contains nerves and blood vessels. The quick is pink colored, but because many dogs' nails are dark, you have to make an educated guess as to where the quick begins. If you cut into the quick, your dog will let you know in no uncertain terms—and won't want you near his paws again! He'll also bleed profusely.

Woofs

The **quick** is the portion of a dog's nail with blood vessels that supply the nail.

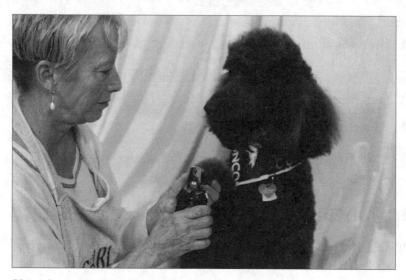

Use either a scissors-type nail clipper (shown), guillotine-style nail clipper, or nail grinder to trim your dog's nails. Be careful not to cut the quick—the pink part that supplies blood to the nail.

When you start clipping your dog's nails, use a dog nail clipper (either a guillotine or scissors style), and snip off a small portion at a time to trim back the nails. If the nail feels "spongy" or hard to cut, stop immediately. You can use a nail grinder, which will help file away the nail instead. Some dogs handle the nail grinder better than the clippers.

Have "styptic powder" or sodium nitrate on hand, in case you do cut the quick. Packing the nail with styptic powder will stop the bleeding. You can buy styptic powder at pet supply stores or through pet supply catalogs.

Anal Sacs

Dogs have two glands at the four and eight o'clock positions around their anus. These usually empty themselves when the dog defecates, but occasionally become overfull or impacted.

If your dog starts scooting around on his rear or chewing the fur on his rear or tail, he may have full anal sacs. The best times to empty these are when you are bathing him. These are smellier than a skunk and you'll want to clean him off after you express them.

To express the anal sacs, fold up a wad of paper towels and place them over your dog's anus. Now press gently on the four and eight o'clock positions. The glands should express themselves. Don't put your face near them while pressing against them or you'll be in for a nasty surprise.

If the problem persists, take your dog to the vet. He could have impacted anal glands, which should be expressed only by your vet.

Dog Treats
The best time to express your dog's anal sacs is during a bath.

The Least You Need to Know

- Your dog will have a healthy skin and coat if he is groomed regularly.

- Depending on your dog's breed and type of coat, he may need grooming every day to once a week to promote good coat health.

- Professional groomers can save you time if you are unable to spend time grooming your dog.

- Don't use groomers who tranquilize dogs, because this can cause serious health problems.

- Keep your dog's ears clean and free from infections by cleaning them with a mild otic solution.

- Get your dog used to clipping his toenails and clip them once a week.

- If your dog scoots on his rear or chews his rear or tail, he may need his anal sacs expressed.

Activities for a Healthy Dog

In This Chapter

- 🏠 Learn how exercise plays a vital role in a dog's health
- 🏠 Learn how to start your dog on a healthy exercise program
- 🏠 Learn what activities you can do

Is your dog a canine couch potato? Like people, dogs who exercise live longer and have a better quality of life than those who just lie around. Like people, dogs love to have a purpose in their lives—they're happy doing a job that's fun and rewarding.

Unfortunately, with today's society, the dog's role has been relegated to that of pet. Many breeds weren't bred simply to be companion animals, hence the conflict. These dogs require work to exercise both their body and mind. Behavioral problems abound in these dogs because they're bored.

In this chapter, I discuss the benefits of exercise for dogs. If you have a dog with problem behaviors, you may wish to pay particular attention to this chapter; it will help you eliminate much of the excess energy that causes bad behavior.

I also cover sports that you can do with your dog. These are just a sampling of different dog sports and are by no means all-inclusive. These activities require just one dog, but you can always expand it to include other dogs if you have a multi-dog household. I cover agility, backpacking, freestyle dancing, flying disc, flyball, and skijoring. I'm certain that you'll be able to find an activity from these that will pique your interest.

The Vet Is In

Dog sports come in all varieties. I cover the following activities in one of my other books, *The Simple Guide to Getting Active with Your Dog* (see Appendix C):

- 🐾 Agility
- 🐾 Backpacking
- 🐾 Canine Good Citizen®
- 🐾 Carting
- 🐾 Dog Shows
- 🐾 Earth Dog
- 🐾 Field Trials
- 🐾 Flyball
- 🐾 Flying Disc
- 🐾 Freestyle Dancing
- 🐾 Herding
- 🐾 Hunting Tests
- 🐾 Lure Coursing
- 🐾 Obedience
- 🐾 Rally-O
- 🐾 Schutzhund
- 🐾 Skijoring
- 🐾 Sledding
- 🐾 Therapy Dogs
- 🐾 Tracking
- 🐾 Tricks
- 🐾 Weightpulling

No Couch Potatoes Allowed!

Doctors constantly nag us about exercising a minimum of three times a week. What's good for us is wonderful for our dogs. What's more, dogs need very little encouragement to exercise. Think about your own dog—doesn't he get excited when it's time for a walk? Imagine his excitement when you're actually going someplace and doing something *with him*.

There are plenty of benefits to exercise. Consider the following benefits:

- Spending more time in an activity with your dog strengthens the bond between the two of you.

- Exercise uses up nervous energy that often becomes undesirable behaviors such as destructive chewing, digging holes, or nuisance barking.

- Exercise is healthy and provides a positive activity.

- Dog sports are fun. Some say "addictive." It doesn't take long when you find your niche before you start buying everything having to do with the activity and start taking road trips with your dog to competitions.

Dog Treats

Before putting your dog on any exercise program, you should have your vet thoroughly examine him. Talk with your vet about the sports you intend to participate in. Your vet may have recommendations concerning diet and conditioning.

Getting Pumped

You wouldn't run a marathon without first training for it, right? (At least, I hope you wouldn't!) Don't expect your dog to do so either. In transforming your dog from canine couch potato to canine athlete, start slowly to avoid injury and overexertion. If your dog is overweight, talk to your vet about putting him on a diet and exercise program. Usually a diet and brisk walk every day is all that's needed to help trim down a pudgy pooch.

Once your dog is trim, you can start adding mileage to your walks. Some people use treadmills made for dogs or use a bicycle attachment, such as the Springer™, to run their dogs while they bicycle.

No Biscuit!

Precautions while exercising:

- Be careful in warm and hot weather—your dog can become dehydrated or suffer heatstroke.
- Pavement and asphalt can cause joint injuries and wear pads thin.
- Offer water frequently.
- Start slow to avoid possible injury.

Agility

Maybe your dog is a superstar athlete, full of energy. If so, maybe agility is to your liking. What is agility? It's one of the fastest growing dog sports. Dogs compete on an obstacle course where they must climb over dog walks, through tunnels, over jumps, and through weave poles. It's exciting to watch and even more fun to participate in.

Types of Agility

Agility is fairly recent to the AKC and UKC, appearing in the mid-1990s. The USDAA (United States Dog Agility Association) appeared in the mid-1980s and NADAC (North American Dog Agility Council) appeared in 1993. All of these sanctioning bodies hold their own "flavors" of agility.

The Vet Is In

Agility debuted in 1978 at the Crufts Dog Show in England. It was intended as entertainment for the crowd between events. Instead, they developed a new sport that has wowed audiences since.

Arguably, AKC and USDAA have the most agility trials of the four sanctioning bodies. USDAA and NADAC tend to have faster courses and require faster times for dogs. UKC places more emphasis on control. AKC agility lies somewhere in between.

Purebreds and mixed breeds can compete in NADAC, USDAA, and UKC agility trials. AKC allows only purebreds. If you decide to try out agility, you'll probably be limited by whether your dog is purebred and what styles are in your area.

Unless you're committed to buying or building all the agility equipment (this is expensive and time-consuming), and have a large enough yard for an agility course, chances are you'll be looking for a professional trainer who has the equipment and the space for an agility course. Those who have equipment usually teach agility training and offer "drop in" lessons for those who wish to practice with their dogs.

The obstacles and course layout vary depending on the type of course offered. In *Standard Class* Agility courses, the course usually has a mixture of *contact obstacles*, tunnels, and hurdles. In *Jumpers Class*, there are usually only hurdles and tunnels. AKC has a special class called *Jumpers with Weaves*, where the obstacles include a set of *weave poles*. Other courses include Gamblers, Snooker, and Relay.

Woofs

Contact Obstacles—A contact obstacle is an agility obstacle that the dog must climb up on and travel across—that is, make contact with. Contact obstacles frequently have zones which the dog must touch to avoid disqualification.

Weave Poles—Weave poles are 1 inch PVC pipe poles in sets of 6 to 12 poles set anywhere from 18 to 25 inches apart in a straight line. The dog must enter the weave poles and weave through them.

Standard Class—In agility, this is a class that has contact obstacles, hurdles, and tunnels.

Jumpers Class—In agility, Jumpers Class has only hurdles and tunnels on the course, making it a very fast course for the dog to travel across.

Jumpers with Weaves—A special class in AKC agility. It is similar to the Jumpers class of USDAA and NADAC, except it has weave poles in the course.

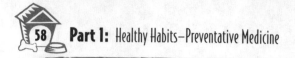
How to Find an Agility Training Class or Club

Agility is a very popular dog sport, so if you live near a city or town, chances are there are agility clubs and trainers in your area. Contact local obedience clubs or training facilities in your area to find out where you and your dog can train in agility. If you can't find a club or training facility, contact the national organizations or surf the Web to www.dogpatch.org and check out their agility calendar. Matches and trials have contact names of the trial secretary, and you should be able to locate a club or facility through them.

The Vet Is In

Shameless plug—If you're interested in learning more about agility, I've written a book on the very subject called *An Introduction to Dog Agility*. Check out Appendix C.

Backpacking

Backpacking in the wilderness is more enjoyable when you take your best friend along. Most dogs enjoy having something to do and carrying their water and treats often add to the dog's usefulness as well as enjoyment. Indeed, thousands of trail miles await you and your best friend.

Any dog in good condition may backpack. If your dog is healthy, free from injuries, joint problems, and bone malformations, he may certainly pack! Even healthy older dogs may pack, provided that you take their age and condition into consideration when exercising. If your dog is a puppy or a young dog, do not backpack him until he is at least eighteen months. Backpacking will stress growing bones and joints and may cause irreparable damage. Ask your veterinarian when you can backpack him safely.

Tell your veterinarian that you intend to backpack with your dog and have your veterinarian thoroughly examine him. Your veterinarian may wish to inoculate your dog against Lyme disease and Giardia and start him on heartworm medication, if he is not already on it. You may wish to discuss tick repellant and first-aid kits for dogs.

Any size dog may backpack, but the usefulness of the dog depends largely on his size. You should not have a dog carry more than one third of his weight, as a rule, without prior conditioning. Most dogs, when starting out, should carry no more than 20 percent of their weight. So, when starting out, a five-pound terrier shouldn't carry more than a pound (including the backpack), and a hundred-pound Malamute should carry no more than 20 pounds. Note that this is a general rule: one pound may be too much for a terrier and you may have to lessen the weight to just a few ounces. The amount of weight depends on the breed and dog's condition. If you have any doubts as to whether your dog can carry the weight safely, reduce the weight immediately. Serious injuries can result from too heavy a load.

> **Dog Treats**
>
> The organization for more information about backpacking and earning backpacking titles is:
>
> Canine Backpackers Association
> P.O. Box 934
> Conifer, CO 80433
> www.caninebackpackers.org

Equipment

You will need your own equipment for hiking. There are many good books and magazines dealing with backpacking, so that will not be covered here. Your dog will need the following items for hiking:

- Backpack—either with or without removable panniers.

- Tracking leash—a cotton webbing leash 10–15 feet long, intended to allow the dog to forge ahead.

- Training collar—either a slip-type collar or martingale-type collar with limited slip. Prong or pinch collars are useful for dogs that pull hard.

- Collapsible water and food bowls.

- Collapsible water containers.
- Dog first-aid kit.
- Dog booties—made from cordura nylon. Useful for protecting worn pads.
- Bags for picking up dog waste.

Flyball

Flyball is a fast, competitive sport where teams of four handlers and dogs compete against each other against the clock. The dogs must jump over four hurdles to a flyball box, trigger the flyball, catch it, and then return over the same hurdles to the finish line and the awaiting relay pair. Teams that complete the relay in less than 32 seconds earn points.

The Vet Is In

The fastest flyball time was 16.70 seconds by a team from Canada.

Flyball Clubs and Competitions

The North American Flyball Association (NAFA) sanctions flyball trials and awards titles to flyball participants. Any healthy dog of purebred or mixed breed can compete in flyball. Dogs obtain titles depending on the number of points. The height of the flyball hurdles depends on the smallest team member. The hurdles are set 4 inches shorter than the smallest dog on the team (minimum 8 inches and maximum of 16 inches), so dogs 12 inches and under are usually welcome additions to flyball teams.

Equipment

Flyball requires the following equipment:

- Flyball box. Plans are available in Flyball books and on the Internet, or you may purchase a flyball box from an obedience supplier.

🏠 Four specially constructed Flyball hurdles.

🏠 Tennis balls.

Flying Disc

Playing Frisbee™ or playing catch with a flying disc is so much more fun when you play with your best friend. Your dog probably already knows how to fetch and bring tennis balls and other items, so why not add a flying disc to his growing repertoire?

Any healthy dog with good structure can become a flying disc dog. There are no requirements for purebred or mixed breed, so any dog is eligible to compete in flying disc competitions. Even if you decide not to compete, flying disc is a great way to exercise your dog.

There are both professional and amateur competitions for flying disc events. These events are put on both regionally and nationally and include The Flying Disc Dog Open™, ALPO Canine Frisbee Disc Championships, and the Quadruped™.

If you enjoy playing fetch and catch with a flying disc and love showing off, consider trying competition. In competitions, you can show off your dog's talent in one of many different venues of flying disc competition:

🏠 Accuracy—The handler must throw the flying disc so the dog will catch the disc within a circle.

🏠 Fetch and Catch—The dog and handler must perform as many completed catches as they can in an allotted time.

🏠 Freestyle—The dog and handler perform their routine to music.

🏠 Obstacles—The handler must throw the flying disc through or over specific obstacles and the dog must catch the disc.

🏠 Long Distance events—These may either be done in teams or solo. In the team events, the competition goes for the longest throw/catch and the team with the short throws are eliminated. Qualifying teams compete against each other and are eliminated until there is a winning team. In solo events, the longest throw/catch wins.

Freestyle Dancing

Do you enjoy dancing, but your counterparts tend to be all feet? Maybe your perfect dance partner isn't human, but your four-footed companion. Freestyle allows you to dance with your dog and have fun. More than just heeling to music, freestyle incorporates a variety of subtle and intricate moves. Freestyle is fun for both you and your dog.

Freestyle is a relatively new sport, appearing in the 1990s. The very first Freestyle routine was developed by Val Culpin in British Columbia, Canada, and was performed by Dawn Jecs with her Border Collie, Checkers, in 1989. In 1991, Musical Canine Sports International (MCSI) was founded in Canada with Ventre Advertising (Patti Ventre) as its promoter. The beginnings of the World Canine Freestyle Organization (WCFO) appeared from this union with Patti Ventre as promoter and president. MCSI eventually evolved into WCFO. Officially, WCFO was founded in June 1999. Another organization, Canine Freestyle Federation (CFF), holds Freestyle events as well.

The Vet Is In _____
The website address for the WCFO is:
www.worldcaninefreestyle.org

Any breed or mixed breed may participate in freestyle competitions. You can have multiple dogs and partners or you may dance with just one dog. Creativity is paramount in Freestyle Dancing.

Skijoring

Do you hear the call of the wild, but only own one or two dogs? Maybe you watch the Iditarod with rapt attention. You can mush, even if you only have one dog. Skijoring is a sport where the dog pulls the owner who is on skis.

If your dog is healthy and over thirty pounds, he can be a skijoring dog. A skijoring dog need not be a Northern Breed, but certainly, the drive to pull and the thick double coat has its advantages! But any dog over 30 pounds can pull a person.

Two Left Feet—or Do You Need to Be an Expert Skier?

You don't need to be an expert skier to try skijoring, but knowing how to stop, skate, and pole are all useful things a skijorer should know. One should also know how to fall correctly to avoid injury. If this is your first time on skis or if you are not a good skier, consider taking skiing lessons to learn the rudiments of the sport.

You will need to be able to help your dog pull you, especially if you are planning to compete. Learning to skate and pole smoothly without disrupting your dog's rhythm is very important, especially if you are planning to enter skijoring competitions.

Equipment

Some notes on skijoring equipment:

🐾 You should have your own ski equipment and clothing. Many people prefer cross-country skis because they allow the owner to work behind the dog more easily. However, the type of ski is determined strictly by your preference and your overall ability.

🐾 You will need a skijoring belt or harness. This type of belt or harness can be made from leather or nylon. It should be padded for your comfort and have a quick-release snap in case you must quickly free yourself from your dog.

🐾 You will need a towline and shockcord. The towline is made from spliced polyethylene rope that attaches one, two, or three dogs to the skijorer. It should be long enough to provide a safe buffer zone for your dog in case you lose control. The shockcord, constructed from bungee, attaches to the towline and protects the dog from hard jolts.

The Vet Is In

Skijoring suppliers:

Adanac Sleds and Equipment
P.O. Box 76
Olney, MT 59927
406-881-2909
www.adanacsleds.com

Alpine Outfitters
P.O. Box 1728
Marysville, WA 98270
360-659-3800
www.alpinehusky.com

Chinookwind Outfitters
P.O. Box 218
Conifer, CO 80433
303-679-9497 or Toll-free
1-866-626-1099
www.chinookwind.com

🐾 Your dog will need an X-back or H-back racing harness. These are the same harnesses used by mushers.

🐾 Your dog may need booties to protect his paws from snow-balling and abrasive snow.

🐾 You may wish to purchase a dog coat for extremely cold weather or if your dog has a short coat.

The Least You Need to Know

🐾 There are numerous activities you and your dog can enjoy.

🐾 When starting to exercise, start slow and build up. Be certain to have your vet examine your dog before starting any exercise.

🐾 Sports that you and your dog can participate in include agility, backpacking, flyball, flying disc, freestyle, and skijoring.

Part 2

Trendy Pup:
Trends in Dog Care

Veterinary care has grown by leaps and bounds. Pacemakers, hearing aids, MRIs, and other high-tech advances have made their way into vet care.

In Part 2, we take a peek at veterinary medicine of the future—vaccines that affect DNA and have virtually no side effects, nutriceuticals, and cutting-edge surgery. But we'll also take a step back and look at another growing trend in veterinary medicine: holistic medicine. Can twenty-first century medicine find room for alternative medicine? The answer may surprise you.

We'll also take a look at pet health insurance. With the high cost of trendy medicine, pet health insurance may be able to cover some unusual procedures. But health insurance doesn't cover everything, and there are pitfalls to avoid.

How Much Does It Cost? The Lowdown on Pet Health Insurance

In This Chapter

- 🏠 Understand why veterinary care is so doggoned expensive
- 🏠 Learn what types of policies are available for dogs
- 🏠 Identify the alternatives to pet health insurance
- 🏠 Learn how to choose the right health insurance for your dog

If you've ever taken your dog to an emergency room or had tests or a nonroutine procedure performed on him, you know vet work is expensive. If your dog needs expensive surgery or treatment for cancer, those bills will skyrocket to several thousands of dollars.

In this chapter, you'll learn why vet care is expensive. You'll also learn about pet health insurance and the pros and cons to getting such insurance. You'll learn alternatives to buying pet health insurance and how to choose the right health insurance for you and your dog.

Why It Costs So Much

One trip to your vet and you may be wondering why pet health care costs so much. A simple checkup and vaccinations may cost $50 or more. Have a series of tests run or an operation, and you're likely to see a bill in the hundreds of dollars. Some operations and care go into the thousands of dollars.

The truth is that vet care is cheaper than the equivalent human health care—yet it requires the same expertise. Nowadays, vets are doing some pretty high-tech stuff at a fraction of the cost. Pacemakers, dialysis, heart surgery, MRIs, and bone grafts are some of the technology in today's veterinary arsenal. If you compare the cost of the last time you went to see the doctor (what your insurance paid) with what your vet charges, you'll see that vet care is relatively affordable. Vets consistently price their services with what they think their clients can pay.

Dog Treats

Pet health insurance can help pay for medical bills that dog owners may not be able to afford.

The Vet Is In

Pet owners routinely spend over $12 billion annually in veterinary health care.

Most vets aren't rolling in money. A vet is a professional and his schooling is just as intensive as a doctor's. Your vet has a practice to pay for, including the business space, the equipment, and the cost of supplies. Believe it or not, he also probably has a family to support, too.

Even so, this isn't much comfort when you discover that to aggressively treat the cancer in your beloved pet, you may pay well over a thousand dollars. Faced with euthanizing their dog or facing a bill they can't afford, many dog owners have sadly opted for euthanasia. I know, because I've had to make that dreadful choice. Luckily, there are options for the pet owner, including pet health insurance.

Talk finances with your vet. If you're a long-time customer, many vets are willing to offer some type of financing option or maybe a payment plan. Not all vets will do this, but if you don't ask, you won't know.

© Margaret H. Bonham

Your vet has a practice to pay for, including his business space, the equipment, and the cost of supplies.

Pet Health Insurance

Pet health insurance started back in 1980 with the advent of Veterinary Pet Insurance (VPI). Since that time, various pet health insurance companies have appeared, some offering what amounts to major medical, others offering a preventative plan, still others offering discounts on certain plans and services.

Health insurance companies come and go, so if you decide to purchase a plan, be certain to choose an insurance that is underwritten by a company rated A or higher. Longevity is also important

> **Dog Treats**
> Purchase your health insurance plan while your dog is young. Premiums increase with the age of the dog.

to consider. The worst thing that could happen is that you pay for insurance and the company goes out of business before you can get a claim paid. It's a good idea to have a second choice in case your first choice goes under.

The Vet Is In

Here are a few of the leading pet health insurance companies:

Pet Assure
10 South Morris Street
Dover, NJ 07801
1-888-789-PETS (7387)
e-mail: custserv@petassure.com
www.petassure.com

PetCare Insurance Programs
P.O. Box 8575
Rolling Meadows, IL 60008-8575
1-866-275-PETS (7387)
e-mail: info@petcareinsurance.com
www.petcareinsurance.com/us

Pet Plan Insurance (Canada)
777 Portage Avenue
Winnipeg, MB R3G 0N3 CANADA
905-279-7190
www.petplan.com

Petshealth Insurance Agency
P.O. Box 2847
Canton, OH 44720
1-888-592-7387
www.petshealthplan.com

Premier Pet Insurance Group
9541 Harding Boulevard
Wauwatosa, WI 53226
1-877-774-2273
www.ppins.com

Veterinary Pet Insurance (VPI)
P.O. Box 2344
Brea, CA 92822-2344
1-800-USA-PETS
www.petinsurance.com

In the previous "The Vet Is In" sidebar, I've listed several plans that are available as of this book's publication. This is not an endorsement of any of their products or plans.

What Pet Health Insurance Covers

Depending on the type of insurance, most pet health insurance covers major catastrophes such as accidents and illnesses. VPI, PetCare, and Petshealth are major medical health insurance plans, covering accidents and illnesses as well as office calls, lab fees, x-rays, surgery, and general treatment. Most of these treatments have a cap, so the payout for cancer, for example, may be limited to $3,000.

No Biscuit!

Pet health insurance companies come and go. Be certain if you purchase a policy that you purchase it with a reputable agency that is underwritten by a well known insurance company and that has a high A.M. Best rating.

Some health insurance plans offer vaccinations and routine medical care either at a discount or for an extra fee. VPI, for example, offers vaccinations and routine care for a set price above the standard premium. Petshealth offers two wellness programs that offer various degrees of preventative care.

Many pet health insurance companies don't cover preexisting conditions or hereditary or congenital defects such as hip dysplasia, entropion, or other potentially expensive problems (see Chapter 10).

Dog Treats

Your vet may be able to work with you on managing the cost of your dog's health care. Some vets offer savings plans or their own form of medical insurance.

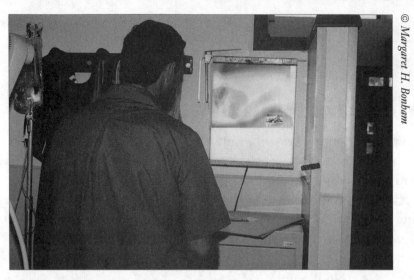

Diagnostic tests can cause your veterinary bill to become very expensive. Pet health insurance may cover these expenses.

Discount Veterinary Clinics

An alternative to pet health insurance, discount vet clinics offer routine services at a discount price. Some of these clinics are available through retail pet supply stores such as PETsMART or maybe a separate discount chain. These vet clinics offer inexpensive vaccinations, heartworm tests and preventative, and low-cost spay and neuter services.

Discount veterinary clinics are good for routine care, but seldom can handle emergencies, surgeries, x-rays, or other diagnostic procedures. Because many of these facilities are staffed with vets who are usually temporary, your dog may not see the same vet the next time you schedule an appointment.

Your vet may be able to match the prices of these discount vet clinics, especially when it comes to a multi-pet discount.

How to Choose the Right Pet Health Insurance for You

When shopping around for pet health insurance, consider asking the following questions:

- How long have you been in business? Who underwrites your insurance and what is the A.M. Best Co. rating? (The higher the grade, the more financially secure the company.) Ratings are from A++ to F. Secure Best's ratings are B+ or better.

- What benefits does your policy offer? Is there a limit or cap on the amount of service? If so, what? Ask for a detailed benefit schedule.

- Does your policy cover *well-ness care* (such as vaccinations, checkups, teeth cleaning)? How much more is it than your basic policy?

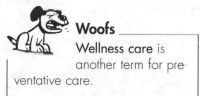

Woofs

Wellness care is another term for preventative care.

- What is the deductible on each policy? (The deductible is your out-of-pocket expense before the insurance begins to pay.) Is the deductible per year or per incident? What is the percentage payout after the deductible?

- Do you offer a multi-pet discount? How much is that discount?

- Does the premium increase with the age of the pet? Do you have age limits on your policy?

- Do you offer discounts on pet supplies and services?

- Does your policy cover pre-existing medical conditions and hereditary and congenital conditions?

- Can I take my dog to any vet or do I have to bring him to certain approved vets?

🏠 What happens to my premium if the company goes out of business?

🏠 What is the payment plan for the premium? (Monthly, quarterly, biannually, or yearly?)

🏠 Do I file a claim or does my vet file the claim?

🏠 How quickly do you pay on a claim?

How much insurance you get depends on the health, breed, and age of your dog and what services you're looking to have covered. Some vets offer veterinary savings plans (similar to medical savings plans) that you can take advantage of. Other vets offer discount cards where you pay to use a certain number of services and get a substantial discount.

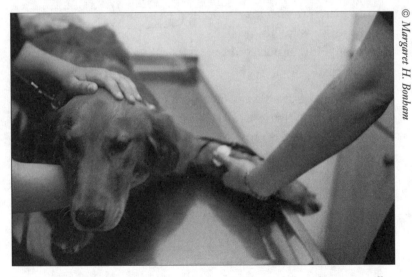

© Margaret H. Bonham

Most pet health insurance won't cover pre-existing conditions, but some will cover routine care.

The Vet Is In _____

The top 10 most frequently submitted claims for dogs in 1999 according to VPI:

Ear infection

Stomach upset

Skin irritation

Tumors or growths

Skin infection

Urinary tract infection

Arthritis

Hypothyroidism

Enteritis (inflammation of the intestinal tract)

Soft tissue trauma (injuries, cuts, and bruises)

The Least You Need to Know

🐾 The cost of veterinary care has risen largely because of advances in pet health care.

🐾 Talk to your vet about finances—sometimes he or she can give you a discount or offer payment options.

🐾 Pet health insurance covers accidents, illnesses, and injuries.

🐾 A few insurance companies offer wellness care such as vaccinations and routine vet visits.

🐾 Choose a pet health insurance underwritten by a company that's highly rated through A.M. Best Co. and has been in business for awhile. The A.M. Best Rating should be no less than a B+ or better.

🐾 Low-cost veterinary clinics and vaccination clinics may help cut down expenses and offer an alternative to pet health insurance.

Chapter 6

Holistic Thoughts

In This Chapter

- 🏠 Learning what holistic medicine is
- 🏠 Determining if holistic medicine is a modern-day form of snake oil
- 🏠 Understanding the major forms of holistic medicine Bach Flower Remedies
- 🏠 Choosing a holistic vet and type of therapy

Alternative medicine has become popular. No doubt you or someone you know has received acupuncture or has visited a chiropractor. Maybe you take nutritional or herbal supplements such as ginseng, St. John's Wort, or glucosamine. You may be surprised to learn that all are aspects of holistic or alternative medicine.

It makes sense that our interest and fascination in alternative therapies would extend to our pets. After all, we want the best care for our best friends. Sometimes we turn to alternative therapy where conventional methods fail or where the "cure" is sometimes worse than the malady.

In this chapter, you'll learn what holistic medicine is and whether it really works. You'll learn what modalities are out there and how to find the best holistic vet for your dog.

What Is Holistic Medicine?

Holistic medicine, often termed alternative or natural medicine, is a popular form of medicine in humans and is gaining ground rapidly in the veterinary community. Unlike conventional or *allopathic medicine*, holistic medicine looks at the whole animal to determine whether something within the dog's entire body might be a manifestation of the symptom. For example, a dog chewing his leg might have allergies stemming from his diet. Rather than treating the dog for the chewing and the rash, a vet would treat the dog by changing his diet. This is an example of how one would look at the whole dog rather than just the symptom.

Woofs

Allopathic medicine is conventional medicine.

Holistic medicine takes into consideration the whole animal instead of simply treating the symptoms.

A **modality** is a form or mode of treatment.

Nutriceuticals are a form of supplementation using natural substances.

Indeed, holistic thinking is starting to permeate conventional veterinary care. More vets are using *nutriceuticals* (glucosamine, creatine, and perna cancalcus mussel, for example) and diet changes to help affect a dog's health. Many well-known veterinary schools are recommending a limited vaccination schedule which includes the administration of certain yearly vaccinations every three years.

Is holistic veterinary medicine a quack science? The answer is more complex than just a yes or no. Because of the lack of hard scientific research, no doubt there are some portions of holistic thought that rank right up there with snake oil. But there are also veterinary medicine advances stemming from holistic medicine that would've been scoffed at 20 years ago. The rest, we just don't know. There hasn't been enough scientific study to determine if some *modalities* are more effective than others—or if they are effective at all.

The Vet Is In _____

Have you worn a magnetic bracelet for pain? Lit a candle to relax? Taken herbal supplements? Visited a chiropractor or acupuncturist? Received a therapeutic massage? Been concerned about what you ate? If so, you have experienced alternative or holistic medicine.

Much of alternative medicine has made its way into mainstream culture. It makes sense that veterinary medicine would explore alternative medicine as well. Naturally!

My own experience is that *some* holistic medicine works. Most holistic medicine can work in conjunction with regular treatment, so there isn't necessarily an "either-or" situation. Most vets are open-minded enough to allow you to use holistic treatments in conjunction with conventional treatments.

The Major Forms of Holistic Therapy

The major modalities of holistic medicine include acupuncture, Bach Flower Remedies, chiropractic, herb therapy, homeopathy, and nutrition. There are other modalities as well, some obscure, some almost mainstream.

No Biscuit! _____

Just because it's "natural" doesn't mean it's safe or better for your dog. There are plenty of natural poisons and harmful substances. Look beyond the term "natural" to find out whether or not the "natural" item does any good.

Furthermore, "natural substances" aren't regulated like medications under the FDA. As a result, nutriceuticals and other holistic remedies may or may not have appropriate potencies.

Acupuncture

Acupuncture is a healing art used by the Chinese for over three thousand years. Veterinary acupuncturists can work on a variety of problems such as arthritis, muscle injury, allergy, autoimmune illnesses, stress, cataracts, and spinal problems. Certification and accreditation is available to veterinarians through the International Veterinary Acupuncture Society (IVAS) and through certain state accreditation boards. (See Appendix B.)

Bach Flower Remedies

Bach Flower Remedies are similar to herb therapy and homeopathy, but address the pet's emotional condition. Dr. Edward Bach discovered these remedies in the early 1930s. There are 38 remedies made from flowers, trees, and special waters.

The Vet Is In

For more information about Bach Flower Remedies, you can visit the Bach Centre Website at www. bachcentre.com. For information on how to purchase Bach Flower Remedies, contact Nelson Bach USA, 100 Research Drive, Wilmington, MA 01887 978-988-3833.

No Biscuit!

Never rely solely on alternative medicine in a life-threatening situation. Much of alternative medicine is not approved by the FDA nor is it proven to be effective.

The most common Bach Flower Remedy is "Rescue Remedy," made from essences of Star of Bethlehem, Rock Rose, Impatiens, Cherry Plum, and Clematis. This is typically used for trauma, shock, fear, and stress.

Bach Flower Remedies are usually given sublingually (under the tongue), in a glass of water, or occasionally dripped on the skin. You can purchase Bach Flower Remedies at a holistic or health food store, or through Nelson Bach, the distributors of Bach Flower Remedies.

Chiropractic

Veterinary chiropractic care deals with diseases caused by spinal interference with normal nerve function. Chiropractors deal with spinal and bone misalignments that can affect organs, muscles, and gait. Certification and accreditation is available to veterinarians through the American Veterinary Chiropractic Association (AVCA). (See Appendix B.)

Herb Therapy

Herb therapy is used to treat a large number of diseases and to maintain the health of the animal. It can be used both internally and externally depending on the type of herb and condition.

Homeopathy

Dr. Samuel Hahnemann, M.D., developed homeopathy in 1790. He discovered that certain substances that produced a disease's symptoms could also cure the disease. By diluting the substance, the healing properties are greatly enhanced and the potential poisonous attributes are removed.

Homeopathy somewhat defies logic. The smaller the amount of substance, the more potent the mixture, according to homeopathists. For a 10x portion of a particular substance, the substance is diluted with water, alcohol, or lactose, and then is diluted in this fashion nine more times. The mixing term is called *succusion*, where the substance is shaken up in a

No Biscuit!

Never give your dog natural supplementation without understanding how the supplement works. Some supplements can interfere with your dog's current medication or may be converted into another substance within the dog's body. Yucca, for example, is a precursor to a steroid and may be converted to a steroid in the body.

Woofs _____

Succusion is the process of diluting and mixing homeopathic medicine.

certain way to release its energy. If you test a mixture, you'll find that none of the original substance remains. Nevertheless, proponents claim that the "energy" of the original substance is still there.

Nutrition Therapy

Nutrition plays a crucial role in your dog's health. Often, holistic vets look for causes of ailments that stem from poor nutrition and allergies to foods as well as pesticides, fillers, and preservatives.

Other Modalities

There are multitudes of other modalities available. Some therapies have been used for thousands of years, others, are fairly recent. Here is a sample of other forms holistic therapy may take.

Aromatherapy

Aromatherapy is the application of scent to facilitate healing. Essential oils can be rubbed into the skin and fur or can be dripped into a cup of warm water and placed near the dog's head.

Biochemical Salts

Biochemical salts, or electrolytes, are salts that exist in living things. Dr. Wilhelm H. Schuessler discovered electrolytes in the nineteenth century. By prescribing these salts or a combination of them, Schuessler treated patients suffering from a variety of ailments.

Iridology

Iridology is a way of diagnosing illnesses and genetic disorders through patterns found in the iris of the eye. By looking at certain markings in the irises, depending on their position and color, those practicing iridology may be able to determine illnesses as they affect certain parts of the body.

Kinesiology

Kinesiology is a method of diagnosing an ailment or testing whether a particular medication will work with a particular animal. A primitive form of biofeedback, it requires the owner to touch the dog and the tester to check the strength in the owner's muscle when asked questions. In testing the medication, the owner must touch the dog and the medication.

For example, a dog named Sasha is limping when brought to a clinic. The vet asks the owner to touch Sasha with her left hand and hold out her right arm. The vet asks, "Sasha, did you injure your foot?" The vet pushes on the owner's arm to see if it is strong or weak. A weak resistance indicates no. The vet then asks, "Sasha, do you have arthritis?" This time, the vet has a hard time pushing down the owner's arm, indicating yes.

The same can be done for medications. The vet has the owner place the remedy on the dog and has the owner touch the dog and the medicine with her left hand. The vet then asks, "Is this the right medicine for Sasha?" A strong resistance indicates yes; a weak resistance indicates no.

Light and Color Therapy

We know that light and color can affect moods. People without enough natural sunlight can suffer from illness and depression. Light and color therapy is used for dogs with emotional and biological disorders, including breeding problems, skin conditions, and other behaviors.

Magnetic Therapy

Magnets have been used to help promote healing of fractures and sore muscles and to alleviate arthritis and joint pain. The magnets are worn either in the collar or on wraps around the afflicted area. Magnets can also be used in blankets or bedding.

Nosodes

Nosodes are the homeopathic version of vaccinations. They are made from infected tissue or other fluids from an infected host. Nosodes are given orally. Because they are intended to prevent disease, but have not definitively demonstrated so in clinical trials, there is some controversy as to whether nosodes are actually effective. There is no clinical proof that nosodes will protect a dog and they are not approved by the FDA.

Pulse Diagnosis

Pulse diagnosis is a method of diagnosing an ailment by taking the pulse along certain energy or meridian lines. As with kinesiology, the tester holds the substance and then tests the pulse again to determine if it is stronger or weaker. A weak pulse suggests the wrong treatment; a strong pulse suggests the right treatment.

Therapeutic Massage

If you've ever had a massage, you know how good you feel afterward. Dogs love massages, perhaps more so than humans because dogs love to be touched and because they can feel an immediate benefit and relief with the massage. Massage is good for injuries and sprains and muscle soreness, and it increases blood flow and helps remove toxins.

 Dog Treats

Look for a licensed veterinarian to treat your dog, regardless of whether he is holistic or allopathic.

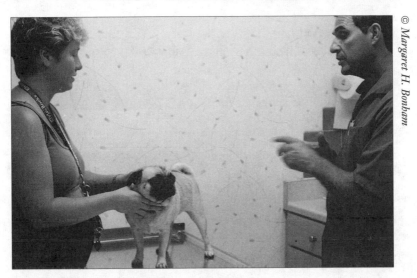

© Margaret H. Bonham

Don't substitute an unlicensed holistic practitioner for your regular vet. Jim Wingert, D.V.M., and client.

How to Choose a Holistic Vet

Choosing a holistic vet is a lot like choosing a regular vet, with some exceptions. Not all holistic vets are skilled in all modalities. You must first decide what modalities you want to use on your pet. For example, if you want a vet who does acupuncture as well as standard allopathic medicine, you will want to contact the International Veterinary Acupuncture Society for a list of approved veterinary acupuncturists in your area and ask whether they practice conventional veterinary medicine.

Once you establish your pet's needs, you can search for the right holistic practitioner. Contact organizations listed in the following "The Vet Is In" sidebar for a list of holistic veterinarians. Ask other like-minded pet owners whom they take their pets to. See if their recommendations correspond with the lists you obtain.

If you go to a holistic practitioner or acupuncturist for yourself, ask them whom they take their pets to. Holistic practitioners often know who is the best in your area for holistic veterinary medicine.

The Vet Is In

National holistic veterinary organizations to obtain for more info:

American Holistic Veterinary Medical Association
2214 Old Emmorton Road
Bel Air, MD 21015
410-569-0795

American Veterinary Chiropractic Association (AVCA)
P.O. Box 249
Port Byron, IL 61275
309-523-3995

International Veterinary Acupuncture Society (IVAS)
P.O. Box 1478
Longmont, CO 80534
303-682-1167

National Center for Homeopathy
801 N. Fairfax #306
Alexandria, VA 22314
703-548-7790

When selecting a vet, be certain to ask questions. Not everyone who claims to use holistic medicine is an expert. Even holistic experts agree that there are charlatans in this field trying to make a quick buck. Choose a licensed veterinarian who has practiced your choice of modalities for many years. Holistic veterinarians use both holistic and allopathic treatments, which can be lifesaving in an emergency or serious illness.

No Biscuit!

Don't substitute an unlicensed holistic practitioner for your vet. While there are many good unlicensed holistic practitioners, there are also many charlatans and people who have good intent, but aren't trained in animal medicine.

Once you've narrowed your choices to veterinarians who practice in your area, call them. Ask about their office hours, modalities used, and accreditations. Accreditations are available through the International Veterinary Acupuncture Society, the

American Veterinary Chiropractic Association, and courses taught
through holistic veterinarians.

The Least You Need to Know

- Holistic medicine has become more mainstream with the accept-
  ance of treatments such as acupuncture, chiropractic care, aromatherapy, massage, herbal supplements, and nutrition therapy.

- Not everything that's natural is safe or healthy.

- Some holistic or alternative therapy works; some doesn't. Most
  is unproven.

- Never rely solely on alternative medicine in a life-threatening
  situation.

- Contact the American Holistic Veterinary Medical Association,
  American Veterinary Chiropractic Association, International
  Veterinary Acupuncture Society, and the National Center for
  Homeopathy for a list of licensed and accredited veterinarians in
  your area that practice the modalities discussed in this chapter.

- Don't substitute an unlicensed holistic practitioner for your vet.

Cutting Edge: Trends in Veterinary Medicine

In This Chapter

- New vaccination technology
- New techniques in diagnosing and treating cancer
- New treatments for epilepsy
- The human-animal bond

Veterinary medicine has advanced considerably, taking cutting-edge technology from human medicine's latest advances. Our four-footed friends have benefited with longer lives and a better quality of life.

In this chapter, I cover a number of advances in veterinary research. These techniques and methods were unavailable to pets and their owners until fairly recently and many are still in the research phase. I cover vaccination technology—what's out there and what's available. With epilepsy, there are new treatments for

dogs with seizures. I cover new advances in cancer research and the human-animal bond and how some medical centers are making euthanasia decisions and pet loss bereavement a little easier.

Breakthroughs in Vaccination Technology

Lately, there have been some new developments in vaccines. As you learned in Chapter 2, vaccines work by introducing a small portion of disease that causes the body to produce an immune reaction. The body produces antibodies that fight against the disease and will protect the dog from the real disease if exposed to it.

Originally, there were only two types of vaccines, modified live vaccines and killed vaccines. In modified live vaccines, a vaccine is made by introducing the disease into an unusual host; aging the vaccine; or modifying the disease through tissue cultures. In any of these methods, the disease is changed enough so that it appears in the dog and replicates just like the disease, provoking the dog's immune system into fighting it, but not contributing to the illness.

In the second type of vaccine, killed vaccines, the dog is injected with the actual disease after it has been killed—that way it can't reproduce in the dog's body, yet the immune system still detects it and reacts against it.

New vaccines, called recombinant vaccines, provide an even greater effectiveness, thanks to the latest genetic research. There are two types of recombinant vaccines: genetic deleted recombinant and live agent recombinant. In genetic deleted recombinant vaccines, the organisms are modified by selectively removing genetic code for virulence factors, thus making the disease harmless. In live agent recombinant vaccines, the genetic code of the disease is inserted into a "carrier" such as bacteria or viruses that pass the disease's genetic code on. Both of these vaccines appear to be more effective than the modified live or killed vaccines.

But it doesn't stop there! Scientists are working to produce vaccines that utilize the disease's DNA or RNA molecules or just its protein. These vaccines will carry virtually no dangerous side effects or allergic reactions. Vets will have to use a special "DNA gun" to inject the DNA or RNA into the dog.

No Biscuit!

No vaccine is 100 percent reliable. Vaccines can fail for a variety of reasons, including:

- 🐾 Handling and administration of the vaccine
- 🐾 The immune response of the dog
- 🐾 The virulence of the disease—some diseases mutate and may render the vaccine ineffective
- 🐾 Maternal antibodies

New Treatment of Cancer

Cancer isn't the death sentence it once was. Nearly 50 percent of all cancers and tumors are treated successfully in dogs using the traditional methods of surgery, *radiation therapy*, and *chemotherapy*.

But veterinary oncologists—veterinarians who specialize in cancer treatment—now have more weapons in their battle against cancer. New procedures enable vets to diagnose the stage the cancer is in and how far it has spread. New drugs allow vets to selectively target the cancer only. And on the horizon are vaccines that may eradicate some forms of cancer.

Woofs

Chemotherapy is the treatment of a disease with medications or chemicals.

Radiation therapy is the treatment of a disease with radiation.

No Biscuit!

Should you try alternative medicine if your dog is diagnosed with cancer? It's best to speak to an oncologist first to determine what course of action is best. Holistic and alternative medicines do not have FDA approval nor are they proven to cure any types of cancer. Often certain cancers when caught in their earliest phases have good prognosis when treated with conventional methods. If alternative methods fail, these cancers can become serious problems left untreated and may not have a cure at later stages.

The best course is to use alternative medicine in conjunction with conventional medicine, but do so only under advisement of the oncologist. Some alternative medicine may actually interfere with the medication or treatment in conventional medicine. For example, antioxidants may interfere with oxidants caused by radiation or chemotherapy intended to kill the malignant cells.

Diagnosing Cancer

Veterinarians still diagnose cancer through standard tests, such as blood work, biopsies, and imaging technologies such as x-rays and ultrasound, but oncology vets are becoming better at determining how far the cancer has spread. In a procedure called *staging*, the vet looks for the disease in other parts of the patient's body to determine how far the treatment must go.

Surgical Techniques

Many cancers and tumors are removed in surgery. Latest advances include laser and arthroscopic surgeries that cause less pain and trauma to the dog. Laser surgery is more accurate than conventional surgery and causes less bleeding. Arthroscopic surgeries aren't as invasive as regular surgery, requiring only a small opening which produces less trauma.

If the cancer is more widespread or malignant, a vet may opt for a combination of treatments with surgery, such as chemotherapy and radiation therapy.

Chemotherapy

Chemotherapy has a bad reputation—but not without some justification: Chemo often targets not only cancer cells, but healthy cells. Even so, certain types of lymphomas can be controlled for up to a year and a half on average using chemotherapy and still provide the dog a good quality of life. Dogs tolerate chemo fairly well: 15 to 25 percent having nausea, vomiting and/or diarrhea and only 1 to 2 percent requiring supportive care.

Rational targeted chemotherapy, a new advance that uses research gleaned from DNA research, may improve these statistics. Scientists have isolated what causes certain cancer cell growth and developed medications that block the cells with abnormal proteins from growing and reproducing.

Radiation Therapy

Radiation therapy is often used in conjunction with surgery or chemotherapy. Treatments can either be with orthovoltage (very low power) or megavoltage (cobalt 60 or linear accelerator).

Some forms of cancer respond well to surgery combined with radiation therapy. Mast cell tumors and soft tissue sarcomas have an 80 to 90 percent success rate with surgery and radiation therapy, even after five years.

Cancer Vaccines

Imagine a day when preventing or curing cancer is as simple as getting a vaccination. Far-fetched? Maybe not.

One leading-edge technology comes from Memorial Sloan-Kettering in conjunction with the Donaldson–Atwood Cancer Clinic at the Animal Medical Center in New York. Dr. Philip Bergman, D.V.M., head of the Donaldson–Atwood Cancer Center

The Vet Is In _____

One leading organization in veterinary research is:

American College of Veterinary Internal Medicine
1997 Wadsworth Blvd., Suite A
Lakewood, CO 80215-3327
website: www.acvim.org

 **Dog Treats** _____

Four great sites to learn more about cancer are the Veterinary Cancer Society at www.vetcancersociety.org, the Animal Medical Center in New York at www.amcny.org, the Morris Animal Foundation at www.morrisanimalfoundation.org, and the American College of Veterinary Internal Medicine (ACVIM) at www.ACVIM.org.

and diplomate of ACVIM (American College of Veterinary Internal Medicine), is leading research there on vaccinations against certain forms of cancer.

The technology makes use of lessons learned in genetic research and molecular technology. Cancer is so insidious because the body often doesn't recognize the cancer cells as being foreign; therefore, the body's immune system doesn't attack them. The cancer vaccine being proposed is made from DNA that appears in another host such as mice or even humans. Because the DNA is from a foreign host, the dog's immune system attacks the vaccine, recognizes the cancer cells already present as being foreign, and attacks the cancer cells. Studies are ongoing but show significant progress, and, at this time, no apparent side effects.

New Treatment for Epilepsy

Most dogs suffering from epilepsy are treated with anticonvulsant medication such as potassium bromide and Phenobarbital. However, new research shows that there may be hope for dogs suffering from severe (unresponsive or recurring) epilepsy.

Research by Dr. Karen Munana, D.V.M., an Associate Professor in the Department of Clinical Sciences, College of Veterinary Medicine, North Carolina State University and diplomate of ACVIM (Neurology), shows promise in decreasing seizures in epileptic dogs.

The Vet Is In _____
Vet medicine has gone high-tech with an online cancer web-site. Even if you live in an area without a vet oncologist, your dog can still get leading-edge treatment. The website www.oncurapartners.com works with your veterinarian to help diagnose and treat your dog. This website is new and allows your vet to access leading oncologists online and even obtain the right medication the next day, no matter where you live.

Studies in humans have shown that ²/₃ of patients have had a reduction in seizures when implanted with a device called a Neuro-Cybernetic Prosthesis. The NeuroCybernetic Prosthesis stimulates the left cervical vagus nerve, which supplies sensation to the ear, the larynx, pharynx, vocal cords, and abdominal muscles, among others as well as motor supply to the larynx and pharynx. Up to a third of the patients experienced a 50 percent or more reduction in seizures. Studies by Dr. Munana indicate that dogs benefit from this device as well.

The vet implants the electrodes around the left vagus nerve in the neck. The generator (about the size of a pacemaker) is placed just under the skin on top of the neck in front of the shoulder blade.

How does it work? Well, researchers and vets aren't exactly certain, but research is ongoing. The cost for this cutting-edge technology as of this writing is about $3,500.

The Vet Is In _____
All human-animal bond programs are offered free of charge. Counselors are available for individual sessions, phone consultation, and support groups. For more info, contact The Animal Medical Center, Human-Animal Bond Programs, 510 East 62 St., New York NY 10021-8383, 212-838-8100.

The Companion-Animal Bond

When is a dog more than just a dog? When he is your closest companion, of course. But at some point in your dog's life you will face

the difficult decision of what to do when he has a life-threatening illness. Should you treat? Should you euthanize?

The plight of the dog owner in this situation is becoming an important issue in veterinary medicine. Top veterinary hospitals such as the Animal Medical Center in New York recognize that decision and grief counseling should be addressed.

The Most Difficult Decision

Although specialized companion animal counselors deal primarily in pet loss and grief counseling, many may be able to help you with euthanasia decisions. At the Animal Medical Center in New York City, Dr. Susan Cohen, D.S.W., the first vet to establish a pet loss support group (in February 1983), offers help so pet owners may evaluate and decide the right course of action for them and their pet. These include ...

🐾 Deciding what course of treatment is best.

🐾 Deciding whether or not to euthanize.

> **Dog Treats**
> Ask your vet for possible pet loss support groups or resources. If your vet doesn't have any recommendations, you can contact local veterinary colleges, humane societies, or even universities or colleges with counselors who are pet lovers.

🐾 Helping to resolve a conflict in the family over a pet because of a medical or behavioral problem.

🐾 Helping the owner understand his or her own feelings on the problem to make the correct decision for their situation.

Often, these counselors have insight into what resources are available to pet owners and can offer choices that the pet owner didn't know he or she had.

Dog Treats

Consider the following questions when faced with a course of action for your dog:

- Is your dog suffering?
- Will the treatment prove beneficial to your dog and improve the quality of his life?
- Can your dog enjoy life?
- Is he able to breathe, eat, urinate, defecate, and move around easily?
- Can you afford the treatment?
- Are you keeping the dog alive for his sake or yours?

In critical decision making, such as whether to treat or euthanize, the owner is often faced with conflicting opinions over what the problem is and conflicting recommendations about what to do about it. Family members, veterinarians, and Internet correspondents may offer different advice.

It helps to speak to an unbiased party who can look at the situation in a nonjudgmental way and offer suggestions to help the owner make the right decision. Animal companion counselors can provide this unbiased opinion.

Dog Treats

Pet loss websites:

- The Animal Medical Center, Human-Animal Bond discussion group at www.amcny.org
- Association for Pet Loss and Bereavement at www.aplb.org
- The Pet Loss Grief Support website at www.petloss.com
- The Virtual Pet Cemetery at www.lavamind.com/pet.html

Pet Loss Support

Grief is natural when one loses one's pet. Some dog owners are closer to their dogs than to many people. Pet loss support counselors understand that in many circumstances, friends, co-workers, and even family members may not be the best people to talk to. Often these people don't understand the special relationship between dogs and their owners. They try to cheer up the grieving person—or worse, tell them that their beloved pet was "just a dog."

Pet loss support groups can help pet owners overcome the overwhelming grief associated with the loss of a pet. Talking with others in the same situation helps owners recognize that they are not alone in their grief and that their feelings are normal.

Dog Treats

Do you know someone who has lost a pet? Here are some suggestions to help them grieve:

- Be a good listener. Let them tell you all about their pet and let them show you photos and pictures.
- Don't try to cheer them up—they've lost an important family member.
- Don't be judgmental. Some statements sound either insensitive or patronizing.
- Send a sympathy card.
- Suggest resources for coping with pet loss.

The Least You Need to Know

- Current vaccination technology includes recombinant vaccines, in which the genetic code of the virus is modified.

- Cancer is not a death sentence in a dog. Approximately 50 percent of cancers in dogs are completely cured.

🏠 Researchers are developing cancer vaccines that may someday cure or even prevent certain forms of cancer in both humans and dogs.

🏠 A new technique for controlling epileptic seizures is to implant a device that stimulates the vagus nerve with electrical impulses. This device is successful in humans and research looks promising in dogs.

🏠 Veterinary centers are recognizing the need to counsel clients in both decision making and pet loss.

🏠 Ask your vet for possible pet loss support groups or resources. If your vet doesn't have any recommendations, you can contact local veterinary colleges, humane societies, or even universities or colleges with counselors who are pet lovers.

Part 3

The Doctor Is In

Even though you take good care of your dog and give him good nutrition, occasionally your dog may still get ill. Learn the most common illnesses and conditions that plague dogs, including parasites. Learn how to win the war against fleas and what works and what doesn't.

In Part 3, you'll learn the common hereditary and congenital conditions in dogs and how to spot them. You'll learn what you need to do to treat minor ailments, but also what to do in case of an emergency.

Last, you'll learn about cancer and tumors, as well as diseases of the older dog. I'll tell you how to make your dog comfortable during his senior years and how to recognize when he has "senior moments." We'll also cover the eventuality of euthanasia.

Chapter **8**

In Sickness and In Health: Common Illnesses and Injuries

In This Chapter

- How to treat many common problems
- Allergies—what causes them
- Diarrhea and vomiting
- Skin and eye problems
- Epilepsy in dogs

Even though you may take good care of your dog, there's still the chance that he will contract some type of illness or injury during his lifetime. In this chapter, I'll cover some of the most common problems dog owners face. You'll learn about allergies and their symptoms and causes. You'll learn about lumps and bumps and how to tell if you should be concerned should you discover one. I'll show you how to recognize common skin and eye problems. As a bonus, you'll even learn how to get rid of skunk odor!

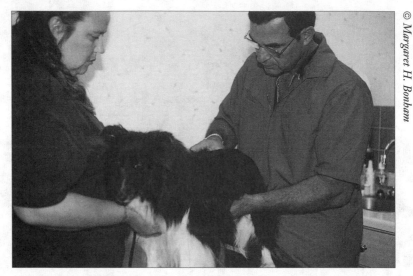

Consult your vet before a problem gets out of hand.

Allergies

Ah-choo! We all think of hay fever when we talk about allergies. You might be surprised to hear that dogs get inhalation allergies, too. But there are other types of allergies dogs get as well, such as contact allergies (allergies to certain external stimuli) and dietary allergies.

Some contact allergies are apparent; some aren't as easy to diagnose. For example, if your dog's skin looks irritated and is itchy after you've washed him with a particular shampoo, you might guess that the dog is allergic to a chemical in that shampoo. However, you might not know why your dog's nose and face are swollen and irritated. Many dogs are allergic to plastic or rubber and may react to the plastic bowls you feed them out of. Most contact allergy diagnoses are based on the owner's observations.

The Vet Is In _____

You may be surprised to learn that lamb isn't any better for a dog than any other type of meat. Lamb was originally used in hypoallergenic diets because dogs had little exposure to lamb meat. However, as more people have fed their dogs lamb and rice diets (thinking that they were better), vets have been seeing allergies to lamb! Lamb is no longer considered a novel protein source for dogs.

Food allergies usually manifest themselves as skin or stomach problems. Dogs can be allergic to certain ingredients in their food such as corn or wheat, or the protein source, such as beef, soy, or lamb.

Dietary allergies are a bit tricky to diagnose. Your vet will recommend a hypoallergenic diet for several weeks. This diet usually has a novel protein source—that is, a protein source that dogs generally don't eat such as fish, venison, or even kangaroo meat. It may have an unusual carbohydrate source, too, such as potatoes. After your dog is on this diet several weeks, you add the potential problem ingredients to determine what the allergy is. Some dog owners are so relieved to have their dogs free from the allergy that they keep them on the hypoallergenic diet.

If your dog is on a hypoallergenic diet, you will have to stop feeding him treats and only feed him the prescribed diet. Many dog treats have the offending ingredients in them. It does no good to put your dog on a hypoallergenic diet if you give him snacks that have the same protein or carbohydrate he is allergic to!

Bad Breath

Contrary to popular belief, dogs aren't supposed to have bad breath. Bad breath is indicative of another more serious problem such as an abscessed tooth or gum disease. You can avoid stinky breath by brushing your dog's teeth regularly and feeding him a high-quality dog food.

If your dog has bad breath, bring him to the vet for a full checkup. Your vet may wish to clean his teeth at that time.

Broken Toenails

Your dog may experience cracked or broken toenails, especially if you allow them to grow too long. Trim the toenail and file off any rough edges if the toenail has broken below the quick (the blood supply to the nail). If the nail is bleeding, you can stop the bleeding with styptic powder, silver nitrate, or an electric nail cauterizer available through pet supply mail-order catalogs. You can then paint the nail with a skin bond agent, which is available from your veterinarian or through veterinary supply houses.

Diarrhea and Vomiting

Changes in diet, overeating, strange water, and nervousness can cause diarrhea, but so can parvovirus, internal parasites, rancid food, allergies, and other serious ailments. If your dog is dehydrated, has a fever (over 102°F), or has extreme or bloody diarrhea, bring him to your vet as soon as possible.

If your dog has mild diarrhea (soft stools—not liquid and without mucus), is not dehydrated, and is not vomiting, you can give him a tablespoon of a kaolin product (Kaopectate) or a bismuth subsalicylate product (Pepto-Bismol). Give 1 to 2 teaspoons per 10 pounds body weight every 4 hours with Kaopectate and 1 to 2 teaspoons per 10 pounds body weight every 12 hours with Pepto Bismol. Withhold your dog's next meal to see whether the diarrhea improves. Encourage your dog to drink water or an unflavored pediatric electrolyte solution. If there is no diarrhea or vomiting, you can feed him a mixture of boiled hamburger and rice at the next meal. If your dog's condition does not improve or becomes worse, contact your veterinarian.

Dogs vomit for a variety of reasons. Sometimes they vomit after eating grass. Dogs also vomit due to obstructions, an enlarged esophagus, parvovirus and other serious illnesses, allergies, and rancid food. If your dog vomits more than once or twice, projectile vomits, starts becoming dehydrated, has severe diarrhea along with vomiting, has a fever (over 102°F), or retches without vomiting, take him to a veterinarian immediately.

The Vet Is In

Occasionally your vet will require you to take your dog's temperature. Purchase an electronic rectal thermometer. Wash the thermometer with soapy water and sterilize it with isopropyl alcohol. Use petroleum jelly as a lubricant and gently insert the thermometer into your dog's rectum. Hold your dog quietly for about two minutes to obtain a reading. Do not allow your dog to sit down or he might break the thermometer or push it farther into the rectum. Normal temperatures for dogs are 100.5°F to 102°F.

Flea Allergy Dermatitis or Flea Bite Dermatitis

Flea Allergy Dermatitis or Flea Bite Dermatitis is caused by your dog's allergic reaction to—you guessed it—fleas (actually, flea saliva). Your dog becomes itchy and his skin becomes red and irritated because of the fleas. Eliminate the fleas and you eliminate the allergy. See Chapter 9 for ways to combat fleas.

Fly Bites

Flies will torment your dog mercilessly during the summer, especially if your dog is an outside or an indoor-outdoor dog. Fly strikes usually occur on ears and face where the skin is most vulnerable. If allowed to continue, flies can actually damage skin; in extreme cases, your dog could lose parts of his ears. Use a mild, roll-on fly ear ointment that can be used in conjunction with any flea and tick pesticides you use normally. Some systemic insecticides do a good job of repelling flies, although the product may not list it as a fly repellant. For more information on systemics and pesticides, see Chapter 9.

Foxtails

Foxtails (or grass awns) are seeds from grasslike plants. They have a sharp, burrowing head with a tail that looks like a fox's tail (hence the name). These seeds have a nasty habit of getting into your dog's fur and ears. With each movement, they burrow into the dog's skin.

No Biscuit!

Check your dog after every time he's been in the field. Foxtails or grass awns can burrow their way into a dog's skin and cause dangerous abscesses. Foxtails have been known to burrow through skin into organs. These are nasty seeds that can do a lot of damage.

Check your dog thoroughly for burrs and foxtails after he's been outside. Check his ears, too. I've seen foxtails bury themselves deeply into a dog's skin. They can cause abscesses and can even enter organs.

If you find a partially buried foxtail, use tweezers to pull it out and watch for signs of infection. Take your dog to the vet if you see pus, swelling, or redness around the site.

Hot Spots

Hot spots are areas of moist dermatitis (skin inflammation) that may become infected. The symptoms are reddening skin, missing hair, and oozing, woundlike lesions. Allergy, matted fur, or some other form of irritation frequently causes them. Shave or clip all hair surrounding the hot spot and clean twice daily with a 10 percent

Betadine/90 percent water solution. If the hot spots are too painful, infected, or extensive, your vet may have to anesthetize your dog to shave the area and prescribe corticosteroids and antibiotics.

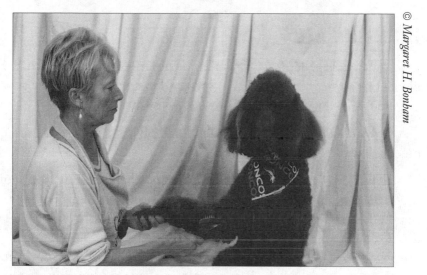

© *Margaret H. Bonham*

Keeping your dog's coat free from mats will help prevent hot spots or moist dermatitis.

Lumps and Bumps on the Skin

Most lumps are usually benign. However, you should show any lump or bump to your veterinarian. Lumps that are oozing, red, dark-colored, irregular in size and shape, or swiftly growing may be serious. If your female dog has lumps on her mammary glands, they may be cancerous mammary tumors requiring surgery. A large, doughy lump on the stomach might be a hernia that your vet may have to fix.

Rapidly growing lumps may be a form of abscess or infection. Abscesses occur when foreign bodies (such as foxtails) enter the skin

No Biscuit!

Rapidly growing lumps that are warm to touch may be abscesses. Have your vet look at all lumps and bumps on your dog.

or an injury closes with bacteria inside. Abscesses are serious. Your vet must drain the abscess and prescribe antibiotics. Do not attempt to drain the abscess yourself; the wound may become more infected.

Incontinence

Incontinence is generally a sign of a more serious problem such as a bladder or urinary tract infection or bladder stones. Have your vet examine your dog to determine the cause of incontinence.

Occasionally, spayed female dogs "dribble" and may require medication to correct.

If your dog crouches down and urinates when you yell at him or touch him, it may be a form of submissive urination. This is a sign that he respects your authority and is submissive. Some dogs are more submissive than others. Scolding or yelling at your dog will only aggravate the problem. You can stop this behavior by remaining calm and speaking quietly. Pet your dog under the chin gently and don't act angry. Most dogs who are overly submissive require some gentle confidence builders such as training and other positive-reinforcement techniques.

Pyometra

Pyometra is a life-threatening infection of the uterus in intact female dogs. It usually occurs about six to eight weeks after the female's last estrus or season. It may come on very suddenly and without warning. Symptoms may be lethargy, refusal to eat, excessive thirst, vomiting, and high temperature. If the cervix is open, you will see a huge amount of blood and pus. If the cervix is closed, you may not see a discharge.

Dog Treats
Spaying your dog will prevent pyometra.

Pyometra is a very serious condition. I lost a female to this disease and I've known others who have as well. No one knows precisely what causes it, other than a hormone imbalance. The usual treatment is spaying, but sometimes the female is so weak that the condition can still kill her. Sometimes vets are able to treat an open pyometra with prostaglandin and antibiotics.

This is yet another reason to spay your female dog. If your dog isn't a show dog or if you're not working her in field trials, you should spay your dog.

Irritated Eyes

Occasionally, you may see redness in your dog's eyes or your dog's eyes might be goopy or teary. Dogs don't cry, so any excessive drainage is most likely due to an eye infection (conjunctivitis), injury, or foreign body.

Your vet can determine the type of infection or whether the dog's cornea has been scratched. He will prescribe the appropriate eye ointment for your dog. Do not use human eye products, as they are made for humans and not for dogs. Human eye products may actually burn a dog's eyes due to improper pH balance.

© Margaret H. Bonham

Consult your vet if your dog has tearing or redness in his eyes. Don't attempt to treat your dog's eyes with human eye medication.

Ringworm

Ringworm isn't a worm, but a fungus. Ringworm causes hair loss, leaving round patches of scaly skin on your dog. It is contagious to humans and other animals, so use disposable latex gloves when treating it. Use a mixture of 90 percent water to 10 percent betadine (available from your veterinarian) to treat the skin. Shampoos and soaps containing iodine also work well.

Dogs can get ringworm from other animals or from the soil. Once it is in the soil, it is very difficult to eradicate. Your veterinarian can prescribe oral medication for chronic or widespread ringworm.

Scratching

Excessive scratching is a sign of a potential skin problem. Examine the area your dog is scratching. Is the skin irritated and red? Is your dog losing hair? Is his skin scaly and flaky? Does he show signs of infestation?

There's a lot of potential problems with scratching. Your dog could be suffering from allergies, Flea Bite Dermatitis, hot spots, or even mange. If his coat is crinkly and dry, it could suggest a potential thyroid problem such as hypothyroidism. Other problems might be unusual such as zinc responsive dermatosis, a hereditary disease that affects Northern breed dogs. (For more information on zinc responsive dermatosis, see Chapter 10.)

If your dog isn't losing hair and is just scratchy (without open sores), perhaps it's time for a bath. There are some good medicated shampoos for dogs to help relieve scratching. Some dog owners like giving a cooked egg or a teaspoon of Canola oil once a week to help improve their dog's coat.

Seizures

Epileptic seizures are frightening to watch, especially if you've never seen them before. There are a multitude of causes for epileptic seizures including some very serious diseases such as rabies and distemper, an imbalanced diet, trauma to the head, brain tumors, hormone imbalance, environmental causes such as chemicals, or heatstroke. However, there are also seizures that are *idiopathic*, meaning we really don't know why the seizure occurs.

There are two types of seizures: grand mal and petit mal. In the grand mal seizure, the dog will go into convulsive fits. He may lose control of his bowels and bladder. He may shake convulsively and whimper or cry out. Usually these seizures last anywhere from a few seconds to less than five minutes. When the dog "comes to," he is usually very disoriented.

Woofs

If a disease or condition is **idiopathic**, its cause is unknown. (A vet once gave me a better definition for idiopathic. According to him, it means that the doctor was an idiot and the patient was pathetic!)

Petit mal seizures are very brief. Sometimes the dog simply "blanks out" or "spaces out" for a few moments. Other times, he may have a sudden facial expression such as a snarl or he may fall over. Again, like a grand mal seizure, the petit mal will leave the dog disoriented.

In rare instances, a seizure may cluster—that is, continue for more than a few minutes. In this case, the dog may suffer brain damage or even death if it is not immediately treated.

I have owned three dogs with epilepsy. It's very disconcerting to see an epileptic seizure the first time. If your dog has a seizure, don't panic. Take him to your vet after the seizure for a checkup to rule out other potential causes. The good news is that just because your dog has a seizure, it does not mean he will have a seizure again. Some dogs have had a seizure and never experienced another one.

What causes a dog to have an idiopathic seizure? Certainly, there are a number of potential causes. Stress may bring on an epileptic seizure, but some dogs only experience seizures in their sleep. Idiopathic seizures in dogs may have a genetic component to them. I had a little female Alaskan Husky who had seizures during her estrus. Spaying her effectively reduced her seizures.

If your dog is diagnosed with idiopathic seizures, your vet may wish to put him on a daily regimen of phenobarbital, primidone, or potassium bromide.

Skunks

There isn't anything much worse than getting skunked! But before you go and buy out the local supermarket's stock of tomato juice, save your money. You'll just get a stinky *pink* dog. Purchase a good commercial skunk-odor remover or use this do-it-yourself baking soda–hydrogen peroxide remedy:

- 1 quart hydrogen peroxide
- 1/4 cup baking soda
- 1 tsp. of shampoo or liquid soap

Wash the dog with the mixture and rinse thoroughly. Don't get any in your dog's eyes. And don't save any of it in a container—it might explode!

The Least You Need to Know

🏠 If you suspect that your dog is allergic to something in his diet, talk with your vet. He or she can prescribe a hypoallergenic diet.

🏠 Frequent vomiting, projectile vomiting, or vomiting accompanying diarrhea requires veterinary attention. Diarrhea with vomiting, that lasts more than one day, is accompanied by a high fever, with blood or mucus in the stool, or with dehydration, requires veterinary attention.

🏠 Spay your female to prevent pyometra.

🏠 Itchy, scratchy skin may have several causes including ringworm, mange, fleas, or hot spots. If your dog's skin is dry, you can bathe him and add a cooked egg or Canola oil to his diet.

🏠 Seizures might have causes or may be idiopathic. Have your vet examine your dog to determine the cause and treatment.

Inside and Out: The Battle of the Bugs

In This Chapter

- Roundworms, hookworms, tapeworms, whipworms, and heartworms
- Giardia and coccidia—two nasty internal parasites
- Fleas and ticks
- Mites

Internal and external parasites can make your dog miserable. Worse than that, they can cause him serious health problems.

In this chapter, you'll learn about both internal and external parasites. You'll learn how to recognize signs of infestation and what the best course of treatment is.

I'll also discuss potential diseases transmitted from these nasty critters. Some of them, such as Lyme, can be transmitted to you if you aren't careful.

Over-the-Counter Dewormers

If you suspect your dog has worms, it might be tempting to treat him with over-the-counter dewormers. Unless you have experience with recognizing worms, treating your dog with medications might not be a good idea. Not all dewormers work on all worms, and some touted for certain kinds of worms may not work well or may have adverse side effects. All dewormers are poisons and even those with a relatively high margin of safety can cause ill effects.

 No Biscuit!

Don't use over-the-counter dewormers on your dog. Many of these dewormers are poisonous if used incorrectly and don't work on all forms of worms. Instead, bring a fecal sample to your vet. He can properly diagnose the type of worms and prescribe the right medication.

It's better to have your dog diagnosed first and the proper medication prescribed by a vet than trying to knock out something that may not even be there.

Roundworms

Roundworms (*Toxocara canis*) are the most common worms among dogs. Puppies frequently contract roundworms from their mothers. If your dog's mother has ever had roundworms during her life, your puppy has probably contracted them. Contracting roundworms is not a reflection of the breeder's care. However, the breeder should deworm the puppies. Roundworms lie dormant in a female dog's body and start migrating to the puppies when the female becomes pregnant. The female can further infect her puppies through her milk. Other avenues for transmission include fecal matter.

Roundworm infestation can be serious in puppies and in old and debilitated dogs. If your dog has roundworms, this means that roundworms are benefiting from food intended for your dog.

Your dog may have a potbelly, may lose weight, and may have a poor haircoat if he is infested with roundworms. Other signs include vomiting, diarrhea, and a garlic odor to the breath. Take your puppy and a fecal sample to the vet. Roundworms can be quite serious and can kill a puppy.

In some instances, roundworms can pass to humans, usually children, and can affect a person's health. The mode of infection is through ingesting worm eggs by touching feces or contaminated dirt and then not washing hands before eating. Roundworms have been known to cause blindness in children.

Hookworms

Hookworms (*Ancylostoma caninum*) are smaller than roundworms and feed off your dog's blood in the small intestine. These worms infest your dog through penetrating the skin or through the dam's milk.

Serious infestations can cause severe anemia and can be life-threatening. Diarrhea, weight loss, and lethargy are also signs of hookworm infestation.

Tapeworms

Tapeworms (*Dipylidium caninum*) are long, flat worms that may infest your dog's intestines. These worms may break off and be excreted in your dog's feces. They look like grains of rice in the feces or around the dog's anus.

Fleas commonly carry tapeworms. Your dog may swallow a flea, thus becoming infested with tapeworms. Other modes of transmission include raw game meat. Some dogs catch and eat mice or other rodents, which also carry tapeworm.

Tapeworms usually do not cause any outward symptoms, but if you see what look like grains of rice around your dog's anus or in his stools, you should have your vet treat him for tapeworms. In rare instances, tapeworms can be passed to humans.

Whipworms

Whipworms (*Trichuris vulpis*) are difficult to diagnose because they don't always produce eggs in fecal matter. These worms feed on blood in the large intestine. Like hookworms, these worms can be serious and cause severe anemia. Dogs become infested by eating something in contaminated soil.

Heartworms

Heartworm *(Dirofilariasis immitis)* is an internal parasite that can kill your dog. Most states within the continental United States have heartworm, although it is less prevalent in the western states.

> **Dog Treats** _____
> It is less expensive and risky to prevent heartworms than it is to treat it. Areas with cold climates require 6 months of heartworm preventative. Warmer areas require that the dog must be on heartworm preventative year-round.

> **Woofs** _____
> Microfilariae are heartworm larvae that infect a dog.

Regardless of where you live, you should have your dog tested for heartworm once a year and put on a heartworm preventative. In many areas, heartworm is seasonal and you only have to administer the preventative during the spring and summer months. Heartworm season is year-round in the southern states and areas where the temperatures seldom reach freezing.

Your veterinarian should administer a heartworm test before putting your dog on preventative. It is a simple blood test that screens for the presence of *microfilariae*, or heartworm larvae.

The Heartworm Lifecycle

Mosquitoes transmit heartworm by feeding on an infected dog. The microfilariae from the infected dog incubate within the mosquito for several days. When the infected mosquito feeds off another dog, it injects the infectious microfilariae into the dog and the dog becomes infected with heartworm.

Preventatives

There are several different heartworm preventatives available, including some that help control other worms as well. Most veterinarians now prescribe monthly heartworm preventatives, although there are still a few daily preventatives available. Do not use the daily preventatives, as they are less effective than the monthly preventatives if administered incorrectly.

There are several types of heartworm preventative. These include:

🐾 **Heartgard (Ivermectin)**   This is the oldest form of monthly heartworm preventative. Heartgard Plus also has pyrantel pamoate for control of roundworms and hookworms. Some dogs (Collies and Shetland Sheepdogs, primarily) are sensitive to Ivermectin, but this sensitivity is rare.

🐾 **Interceptor (Milbemycin) and Sentinel (Milbemycin and Lufenuron)**   Interceptor controls heartworm as well as hookworms, roundworms, and whipworms in a monthly preventative. Sentinel also controls fleas.

🐾 **Revolution (Selamectin)**   A topical application, Revolution works as a monthly heartworm and flea preventative.

🐾 **Proheart 6 (Moxidectin)**   A six-month preventative, Proheart 6 is given as an injection and can be administered only by your vet.

Treatment for Heartworm

Only a veterinarian can treat a heartworm-positive dog. Heartworm treatment is still risky, but is now safer and less painful than the old treatment, which used an arsenic IV solution. Often, the old heartworm treatment was just as dangerous as the heartworm infection. The new treatment requires two injections. If your dog has heartworms, be certain that your veterinarian is using a treatment newer than the arsenic-based solution.

Giardia

Giardia is a microscopic organism that can cause extreme diarrhea and vomiting. Dogs can pick up giardia by drinking water from streams and lakes or other contaminated sources. A person can contract giardia the same way or by failing to wash their hands after cleaning up after a giardia-infected dog.

Giardia symptoms can be mild to extreme. It can be chronic and may reoccur even after treatment. Only your vet can prescribe medications that will cure giardia.

If you contract giardia, you must see your doctor immediately. In some people, diarrhea and vomiting is extreme to the point where they rapidly lose weight and become severely dehydrated and have to be hospitalized. Your doctor will prescribe medications to treat giardia, but this is a stubborn organism and may require more than one treatment.

 No Biscuit!

Don't drink the water in small mountain towns in the Rocky Mountains; drink bottled water instead. Many small towns don't adequately screen for giardia and those with no exposure may find themselves with a nasty case. I've had dogs get giardia from water from contaminated wells. When they have it, you'll *know* it! Also be careful with coffee and tea—most aren't heated sufficiently to kill giardia.

Coccidia

Coccidia are microscopic parasites that frequently affect puppies in crowded puppy mill conditions. Occasionally puppies from reputable breeders may contract it if a dog with coccidia comes in contact with the puppies. Your veterinarian can prescribe medication to treat coccidia.

Symptoms include diarrhea, vomiting, and dehydration.

Fleas

Fleas thrive in all climates except the very cold, the very dry, and high altitudes. If you live in one of these climates, you're feeling very smug right now. If you don't, you're probably looking at a map to find such a place. Fleas are horrible critters and are hard to get rid of once you have them.

If you suspect a flea infestation, search for fleas on your dog around his belly and groin area, at the base of his tail, and around his ears. A common sign of fleas are deposits of black flea feces that turn red when wet.

If you find fleas on your dog, you're certain to have a flea infestation in your home. Talk to your veterinarian about ways to combat the problem. Often, your veterinarian can recommend a system that will combat fleas in the yard, in your house, and on your dog.

No Biscuit!

You may be surprised to learn that flea collars are usually ineffective against fleas because the dog is too large of an area for the collar to cover. Flea collars can also be poisonous, especially if your dog chews and swallows it.

Health Hazards

Fleas are more than just annoying hard-shelled insects that feed on blood and make your dog miserable. Fleas are carriers of tapeworm and bubonic plague, which can cause your dog severe health problems. Bubonic plague is deadly and you can contract it as well as your dog. Fleas carry other diseases, too, so don't consider them just a nuisance.

Declaring War

Once you find fleas, the best thing is to contact your vet for recommendations. Your vet will recommend products based on your climate and your dog's age and health. He will also recommend products that are safe to use together. Be very careful about mixing products and always read the label.

> **Dog Treats**
>
> Slip a piece of flea control collar in the vacuum cleaner's bag to help kill the fleas. Then, throw out the vacuum cleaner bag—you don't want the fleas to find their way back out into your house.

> **Dog Treats**
>
> One vet I know recommends Preventic™ tick collars to prevent ticks from attaching to dogs. It is very effective against ticks, but not against fleas. As with any collar, it can be poisonous if your dog chews and swallows it.

You'll have to vacuum all carpets and furniture—anywhere fleas hide. I've heard of putting a piece of flea collar in the vacuum cleaner bag to kill the fleas.

Systemic treatments (topicals which enter the dog's body and provide complete protection) have made most drastic measures (such as flea bombs, flea powders, etc.) obsolete except in the worst infestations.

Your Latest Arsenal

Some systemic flea treatments are …

- **Frontline (Fipronil) and Frontline Plus (Fipronil and Methoprene).** Treatment works by killing fleas within 24 to 48 hours. Frontline Plus contains an insect growth regulator that keeps immature fleas from reproducing. It is a topical, spot-on systemic that works for three months on adult fleas and one month on ticks.

- **Advantage (Imidacloprid).** Treatment works by killing both adult fleas and larvae within 48 hours. It is a topical, spot-on systemic that works for six weeks on adult fleas.

🏠 **Program (Lufenuron).** Treatment works by preventing flea eggs from hatching or maturing into adults. It is a pill you give once a month.

🏠 **Biospot (pyrethrins and fenoxycarb).** Treatment is a topical spot-on systemic that kills fleas and ticks for one month. It has an insect growth regulator that keeps immature fleas from reproducing. I've also seen it repel flies.

Over-the-Counter Weapons

Be extremely careful when working with insecticides. Insecticides are poisons and can harm your dog if used improperly. Some medications and wormers may react with certain pesticides, so it is very important to be certain that what you are using will not interact with other pesticides or medications. Contact your veterinarian or your local poison control center concerning their safety.

When you do select a system, find one that will work together in your home, in your yard, and on your dog. Many manufacturers make flea control products that are intended to work together as a complete solution.

Ticks

Ticks are nasty relatives of the spider. They can be as large as a button or smaller than a pinhead, but have a bulbous body, small head, and eight legs. Ticks carry dangerous diseases such as Rocky Mountain Spotted Fever, Lyme disease, and Ehrlichiosis. If your dog has been outside for any period of time or has run through deep underbrush, you should check him over for ticks.

Removing Ticks

If you find a tick on your dog, avoid handling it or you may risk exposing yourself to disease. Instead, treat the area with a good tick insecticide approved for use on dogs, wait a few minutes, and then try to remove it. Wear latex gloves and use tweezers. Firmly grasp the tick with the tweezers and gently pull. Don't try to pull the tick out if it resists. You may leave portions of the tick embedded in your dog, which can cause infection. Wait for the tick to drop off and dispose of it.

The Vet Is In

Lyme disease first appeared in Lyme, Connecticut, in 1975. Cases have been reported in most of the continental United States. It is a tick-borne disease caused by the bacteria *Borrelia burgdorferi*. The principle carriers of Lyme disease are the "deer ticks" *Ixodes dammini, Ixodes scapularis, Ixodes ricinus,* and *Ixodes pacificus*. These ticks are much smaller than common dog ticks—most being a little larger than a pinhead. Nymphs (immature ticks) can carry Lyme disease. You may not be able to detect nymphs because of their tiny size (1–2 mm).

Common signs of Lyme disease are lameness and fever. A dog with Lyme disease may lack appetite, be unusually tired, and might have swelling of the lymph nodes. The dog may have bouts of unexplained lameness that may become chronic. It may involve one or several joints. If left untreated, it can cause serious neurological, heart, and renal problems. Your dog can infect you if you handle the ticks or come in contact with your dog's bodily fluids such as blood or urine.

Early treatment offers the best prognosis. The treatment of choice is antibiotics such as tetracycline, penicillin, and erythromycin. There is now a Lyme vaccination available for dogs. If you live in a Lyme-prevalent area, such as the Northeast or upper Midwest, talk with your veterinarian about minimizing your dog's exposure to Lyme.

Identifying Tick-Borne Diseases

Ticks carry a variety of diseases including Lyme disease, Canine Ehrlichiosis, Babesiosis, and Rocky Mountain Spotted Fever. These diseases can greatly affect your dog's health or may even be fatal in extreme cases. Your vet can test for tick diseases through a blood

test and can treat them with medications. If your dog tests positive
for one of these tick-borne diseases, you may wish to consider having your own doctor test you for the same disease. Ticks can transmit these diseases to humans, and in rare instances, contact with
your dog's bodily fluids may transmit these diseases to you.

The following is a list of tick-borne diseases and their symptoms
in dogs. Some of these symptoms are similar in humans, but you
should consult a medical professional for actual symptoms within
humans:

🐾 **Lyme disease.** Common signs of Lyme disease are lameness
and fever. A dog with Lyme disease may lack appetite, be
unusually tired, and have swelling of the lymph nodes. The dog
may have bouts of unexplained lameness that may become
chronic.

Early treatment offers the best prognosis. The treatment of
choice is antibiotics such as tetracycline, penicillin, and erythromycin.

🐾 **Canine Ehrlichiosis.** Common signs of Canine Ehrlichiosis
are fever, discharge from the eyes and nose, and swollen limbs
(edema). A dog with Canine Ehrlichiosis may lack appetite, be
unusually tired, and have swelling of the lymph nodes.

The treatment of choice is tetracycline, or in some cases doxi-
cycline, both of which are antibiotics and must be prescribed
by your vet.

🐾 **Babesiosis.** Common signs of Babesiosis are fever, lethargy,
and lack of appetite.

The treatment is Imitocarb diproponate and must be given by
your vet.

🐾 **Rocky Mountain Spotted Fever.** Common signs of RMSF
are high fever, abdominal pain, coughing, lack of appetite,
lethargy, swelling of face or limbs, depression, vomiting, diarrhea, and muscle or joint pain.

The treatment of choice is tetracycline, which is an antibiotic and must be prescribed by your vet.

Mites

Mites are microscopic arachnids, related to ticks and spiders. There are several types of mites, including those that cause sarcoptic and demodectic mange and those that enter the ears and cause infection.

Ear Mites

Ear mites (*Otodectes cynotis*) will make your dog miserable. If your dog has reddish-brown earwax, he may have ear mites, especially if he scratches or shakes his head frequently. Those floppy ears are great for encouraging mites and bacterial infections, so it is very important to keep your dog's ears clean.

Don't try to treat ear mites with over-the-counter solutions because there may already be a secondary infection. Your vet will need to clean out the reddish-brown gunk and then give you ear drops to kill the mites and handle any infections.

Mange Mites

There are two types of mites that cause mange. Demodectic (*Demodex canis*) mites feed primarily on the cells of the hair follicle. Demodectic mange appears as dry, scaly red skin, with hair loss, mostly around the face. Demodectic mange mites exist on all dogs, but are thought to be triggered by a depressed immune system. Most of the time, localized demodectic mange clears up on its own. If it is generalized or doesn't clear up, it is hard to treat and must be treated by your veterinarian.

Sarcoptic mites (*Sarcoptes scabei*) are highly contagious. This mange may spread quickly in kennels. It manifests as itchiness accompanied by hair loss and a red rash. The dog may have ugly sores from scratching. Your vet can prescribe a topical product to treat sarcoptic mange. You may have to treat your dog with medicated baths and body dips. If the sores are infected, your vet may prescribe antibiotics.

Your vet can diagnose your dog with skin scrapings to determine if he has mites and what type.

The Least You Need to Know

- Internal parasites can cause your dog severe health problems. You should not treat them as normal or commonplace.

- Don't treat your dog with over-the-counter dewormers, as they may be ineffective against certain worms. All dewormers are poisons and dosing your dog with the wrong dewormer or incorrectly may make your dog very sick.

- Heartworm is a dangerous parasite that can kill your dog. There are preventatives that will help keep your dog heartworm-free.

- Fleas are more than annoying hard-shelled insects—they can carry diseases such as bubonic plague or tapeworms, which can be carried to humans.

- Ticks can spread diseases such as Lyme Disease, Canine Ehrlichiosis, Babesiosis, and Rocky Mountain Spotted Fever. You, too, can contract these diseases from ticks.

- There are several types of mites, including ear mites and mange mites. Your vet can make the appropriate diagnosis and treatment.

Chapter 10

"Rampart—Stat!" Emergencies

In This Chapter

- Assembling a first-aid kit
- Muzzling your dog
- Dealing with emergencies

Try as we might to make our dogs' lives safer, you may still have an emergency crop up from time to time. Keep your vet's after-hours phone number or the local emergency vet's phone number handy just in case.

Don't panic in an emergency. Panicking wastes precious time you can use to save your dog. Remember that your dog is in pain and scared—he may snap or bite, even at you.

Assembling a First-Aid Kit

Having a first-aid kit for your dog is important. You can assemble one from easily purchasable items:

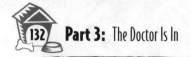

- Aspirin (not ibuprofen or acetaminophen)
- Bandage scissors
- Bandage tape
- Betadine solution
- Cortisone cream
- Disposable latex gloves
- An emergency veterinary hospital's phone number
- Hydrogen peroxide
- Kaolin product (Kaopectate)
- Large and small nonstick bandage pads
- Local poison control center phone number
- Mineral oil
- Petroleum jelly (Vaseline)
- Pressure bandages
- Quick muzzle
- Rectal thermometer
- Self-adhesive wrap (VetWrap or Elastaplast)
- Sterile gauze wrappings
- Sterile sponges
- Surgical glue or VetBond (available through veterinary-supply catalogs)
- Syrup of ipecac
- Triple antibiotic ointment or nitrofurizone (available through veterinary-supply catalogs)

- 🏠 Tweezers

- 🏠 Unflavored pediatric electrolyte (Pedialyte)

- 🏠 Your veterinarian's phone
  number, pager, or after-hours
  number

Dog Treats _____
   Always have your
vet's number, the number to the
local poison control center, and
the nearest 24-hour emergency
vet clinic number taped to your
phone, just in case.

How to Muzzle Your Dog

In an emergency, you may have to muzzle your dog. Even the gentlest dog may bite if frightened or injured. Have a quick muzzle (sold
in pet-supply stores and through mail order) available. If you don't
have one, you can fashion a makeshift muzzle from a bandage, a
rope, a belt, or a tie.

Follow these steps to muzzle your dog:

1. Start in the middle below the dog's muzzle.

2. Wrap the bandage upward,
   tie, and then bring it back
   downward under the chin
   and tie.

3. Take the two loose ends and
   tie them behind the dog's
   head securely.

No Biscuit! _____
   Do not muzzle a
dog who is having problems
breathing, is overheated, or that
has a sucking chest wound.

How to Give the Dog Mouth-to-Mouth Resuscitation

If your dog has stopped breathing, perhaps the only way to save his
life is to give mouth-to-mouth resuscitation. Start by removing the
dog's collar and any other constricting device and make certain your

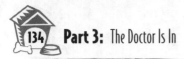

dog's airway is clear. Close his mouth, hold his jaws together, and blow gently into his nose. Don't blow hard or over-inflate his lungs or you may rupture a lung. His side should move as if he were breathing normally. Now release and let the air leave the lungs. Breathe in again and release. Continue to do this until your dog is breathing on his own.

Broken Bones

Fractures to the head, chest, or back, as might occur when a dog is hit by a car, may be life-threatening. Use a stiff board to transport the dog (slide the board under the dog) and seek immediate veterinary attention. If your dog has broken his leg, you can fashion a splint from a stick, a rolled-up piece of stiff cardboard, or even a rolled-up newspaper. Put the splint alongside the broken leg and wrap either VetWrap or tape around it. Transport your dog to the veterinarian as soon as possible.

Burns

A severe burn (where the skin is charred or where underlying tissue is exposed) requires immediate veterinary attention. You can treat minor burns over a small area with ice packs or cold water. Do not use water on extensive burns or the dog may go into shock. Aloe vera is a good burn treatment after the burn has blistered.

Choking or Difficulty Breathing

Signs of choking and breathing difficulty include gagging, coughing, gums and tongue turning pale or blue, and wheezing. Do not muzzle your dog, and seek immediate veterinary attention. Loosen your dog's collar and anything else that might restrict breathing. Check your dog's throat for any object caught in the throat. If you see something that you can remove with tweezers, do so. Do not use

your fingers; you can accidentally push the item farther down. If the item is lodged in the throat, try pushing on the dog's abdomen right beneath the rib cage to expel the object.

If the dog is not breathing, give it mouth-to-mouth resuscitation by closing the dog's mouth and breathing into its nose. (See "How to Give the Dog Mouth-to-Mouth Resuscitation," earlier in the chapter.) You could ask your veterinarian how to perform mouth-to-mouth resuscitation correctly, as well as cardiopulmonary resuscitation (CPR).

> **Dog Treats**
> Ask your vet to show you the proper way to perform CPR on a dog.

Cuts, Injuries, and Bites

You can clean minor cuts and scrapes yourself with a 10 percent Betadine/90 percent water solution. Then apply a triple antibiotic ointment and watch for signs of infection. Seek veterinary attention if you see signs of reddening, inflammation, or signs of infection such as oozing pus.

Severe cuts and lacerations will most likely require suturing. Use pressure bandages to slow or stop the bleeding, except in severe crushing injuries, and take the dog to a vet. If injuries are internal, as from a car accident, there may be internal bleeding. Use a stiff board to transport and seek veterinary attention.

In the case of arterial bleeding, the blood is bright red and sprays out with each heartbeat. Use pressure bandages and apply pressure directly to the artery. Seek immediate veterinary attention.

For deep puncture wounds, determine how deep the puncture is. If the object is still embedded, do not remove if practical, and seek immediate veterinary treatment. If you remove the object, you may cause more serious bleeding than if you left it in, so do not remove unless absolutely necessary. If the puncture is a bite that is

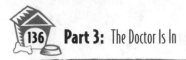

not serious, you can clean the wound with a Betadine/water solution. Your veterinarian might want to prescribe antibiotics to prevent infection. If the dog was bitten by another dog, be certain that both your dog and the biting dog have had their current rabies vaccinations.

Cut pads tend to bleed badly. Staunch the bleeding with styptic powder and then apply an antibiotic to it. You can wrap the foot with gauze and put a bootie on, similar to those you can buy at a pet supply store or from a sled dog outfitter. (Booties.com is one possible source.) If the cut or split is minor, you can take a piece of leather a little larger than the cut on the pad and affix it to the pad using surgical or super glue. This will help the pad heal.

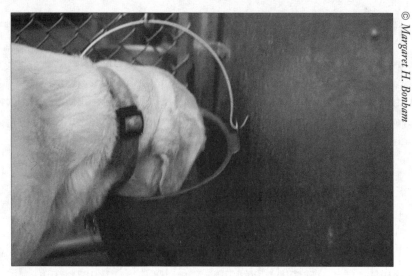

© *Margaret H. Bonham*

Water is important to prevent dehydration.

Dehydration and Heatstroke

Dehydration, that is, the loss of water in a body, can occur during any season. Heatstroke usually occurs in hot weather, but may happen at any time if the dog's breathing is restricted or if kept in a confined area without good ventilation.

Signs of dehydration and heatstroke include elevated temperature, extreme thirst, watery diarrhea, vomiting, lethargy, high temperature (over 103°F), skin around muzzle or neck that does not snap back when pinched, difficulty breathing, weakness, and pale gums.

Do not muzzle a dog who is suffering from dehydration or heatstroke. Move dog into shade or a cool and well-ventilated area. Give your dog cool water or unflavored pediatric electrolyte to drink. Soak the dog in tepid or cool water. Do not use ice-cold water, as it will cause the capillaries to contract and not dissipate heat. Make certain the dog can breathe—remove constricting collars or other items. Obtain immediate veterinary attention.

Prevent heatstroke by keeping your dog in well-ventilated areas with shade in the summertime. Always provide fresh water. Do not exercise your dog in hot weather. Never leave a dog in a car during warm weather even with the windows down.

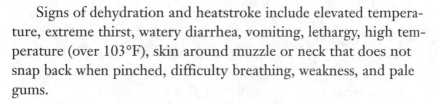

No Biscuit!
Never leave a dog in a car during warm weather—even with the windows rolled down. It takes very little time for the temperatures to become deadly within a hot car.

Drowning

Contrary to popular belief, not all dogs are good swimmers and even dogs that are good swimmers can become tired and drown, especially in swimming pools, where they may not learn how to get out.

Lay the dog with his head downhill so that the water can drain out of his mouth and lungs. Press gently on his abdomen, just below the rib cage, to make certain that the water is gone. If he is not breathing, try mouth-to-mouth resuscitation and CPR. Seek veterinary attention immediately.

If you have a swimming pool, consider keeping your dog away from it to avoid possible drowning. Most dogs don't know how to get out of a pool once in. Teach your dog how to walk out of the pool through the shallow area so that he knows how to get out if he ever accidentally gets into the pool.

Electrical Shock

Dogs love to chew, and unfortunately electrical cords pose a serious risk. Teach your dog to stay away from electrical cords and keep them out of reach at all times.

If your dog chews an electrical cord and gets shocked, do not touch your dog or you might be shocked also. Use a wooden broom handle or other nonconductive item to unplug the cord. Treat as you would for traumatic shock by maintaining proper body temperature and seek emergency veterinary treatment. If the dog is not breathing, administer mouth-to-mouth resuscitation by closing the dog's mouth and breathing into its nose.

Fishhooks

Fishhooks are nasty. If your dog has stepped on one or had one pierce her lip, take her to a vet. If no vet is available, you may have to muzzle your dog and look for where the hook's barb is. Push the

barb through the skin if necessary to expose it and then snip it off with a pair of wire cutters. Then remove the hook. Contact your vet; he or she may wish to prescribe antibiotics. Only your veterinarian should remove swallowed fishhooks.

Frostbite and Hypothermia

Hypothermia occurs when a dog's body temperature becomes very low. More than just being cold, it means a dog cannot warm himself to survive. Signs of hypothermia include lowered body temperature, shivering, and lethargy, followed by stupor, shock, unconsciousness, and finally death. Lack of food for energy and dehydration can greatly affect your dog's ability to keep warm. Dogs expend energy and heat while working, but if the heat loss is too great, your dog may experience hypothermia.

Treatment for hypothermia is mostly common sense. Warm your dog slowly by wrapping him in blankets or lying next to him in blankets to help warm him. If he is conscious, you should offer him warm broth (beef or other meat juices with water) to drink. Seek immediate veterinary attention.

Frostbite is skin damage as a result of cold. The skin will turn white if frostbitten. If severely frostbitten, the skin will turn black. Sometimes the affected skin will slough, leaving a raw sore. If the skin is white and intact, warm it slowly in tepid water (not hot—you can damage the skin further). It will be painful to warm the skin. In frostbite with sores, wrap with an antibiotic ointment and gauze. In all cases of frostbite, seek veterinary attention.

Insect Bites and Stings

You can treat most insect bites and stings with an over-the-counter antihistamine (such as Benadryl) that your veterinarian can recommend. If your dog shows any allergic reactions to bites or stings

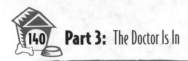

(severe swelling or difficulty breathing), seek immediate veterinary attention. This can be a life-threatening condition known as an anaphylactic reaction.

The Vet Is In _____
The Brown Recluse can be recognized by an M-shaped marking on its back.
The Black Widow spider is black with a characteristic red hourglass on its abdomen.

Spider bites can be very serious. The two most dangerous spiders are the black widow and the brown recluse. Black widows are found everywhere in the United States, but the brown recluse is generally found in warmer areas. Both of these spider bites can be fatal if left untreated. If you suspect a spider has bitten your dog, seek veterinary attention.

Poisoning

There are many different poisons your dog can get into. Some are ingested, like antifreeze or chocolate, but some your dog may come in accidental contact with, such as insecticides or fertilizers.

Contact your veterinarian or local poison control center and have available the substance or chemical that your dog has ingested so that you can properly describe the poison. Follow the veterinarian or poison control center's instructions. Do not induce vomiting unless told to do so. Some acids, alkalis, and other substances can harm your dog more if they come back up.

No Biscuit! _____
It your dog has swallowed something poisonous, *do not induce vomiting* unless the vet or poison control center tells you to do so.

The Least You Need to Know

- Realize that most emergencies require veterinary attention, but you can do things to help improve your dog's chances of survival.

- Muzzle your dog—except when he has trouble breathing—to avoid being bitten.

- Remember, even the gentlest dogs may bite if scared or injured.

- Know that a first-aid kit for your dog is handy when emergencies come up.

- Ask your vet the correct way to perform CPR and mouth-to-mouth resuscitation.

Chapter 11

Congenital and Hereditary Diseases

In This Chapter

- 🏠 Understand what congenital and hereditary diseases can affect your dog, be he purebred or mixed breed
- 🏠 Learn about common hereditary diseases such as hip dysplasia, elbow dysplasia, and eye problems
- 🏠 Identify other, breed-specific congenital and hereditary diseases

While reputable breeders go to great strides to eradicate genetic diseases in their lines, other breeders, puppy mills, and backyard breeders are breeding dogs haphazardly and perpetuating poor health.

Some genetic diseases can be screened for successfully. For example, reputable breeders have screened for hip dysplasia, effectively reducing or eliminating the numbers of dysplastic dogs in their lines.

In this chapter, you'll learn about *congenital* and *hereditary* conditions that afflict dogs.

> **Woofs**
>
> A **congenital** disease is one that is present at birth and may have either genetic or environmental causes.
>
> A **hereditary** disease is one that is genetic, that is, inherited through the genes of the parents.

Bloat (CGDV)

Bloat—also called gastric torsion, gastric dilatation, or canine gastric dilatation-volvulus (CGDV)—is a life-threatening condition. Body structure seems to be the main determinant as to whether a dog will bloat; it affects many large, deep-chested breeds, including Labrador Retrievers, Great Danes, German Shepherd Dogs, and Sighthounds, among others.

> **No Biscuit!**
>
> Watch for signs of bloat: suddenly looking fat or "pregnant," pacing and drooling, discomfort when sitting or lying down, and retching and attempts at vomiting without producing anything. Bloat is a life-threatening condition—seek veterinary attention immediately.

The afflicted dog's stomach fills with gas and fluid. More than just an upset stomach, the dog's stomach fills so much that it begins to twist on its axis. This terrible twisting damages the stomach, esophagus, and intestines, and shuts off blood supply to those organs. When the stomach twists, the condition then is called gastric torsion or gastric dilatation-volvulus (CGDV). If untreated, the dog will go into shock and die a painful death.

Bloat occurs up to three hours after eating. Your dog will suddenly look pregnant or fat. He may pace back and forth and look uncomfortable. He may drool and attempt to vomit without success. If your dog shows these symptoms after eating, don't attempt to treat him yourself! Get him to the vet as soon as possible.

Commonly affected breeds: all large and giant breeds.

> **Dog Treats**
>
> The best treatment for bloat is to prevent it. Here are some tips:
>
> - Feed him several smaller meals rather than one big one.
> - Wet down your dog's food (don't let it sit long) to encourage quick evacuation from the stomach. Tests show that food with water poured over it leaves the stomach less than an hour after eating.
> - Don't change dog foods or give snacks that cause digestive upset.
> - Don't exercise your dog after he has eaten. Give him an hour or so before exercising again.
> - Encourage slower eating. Some people have gone as far as to put fist-sized stones (too big for their dog to accidentally swallow) in their dogs' bowls to encourage them to slow down.
> - Don't allow garbage raids, counter raids, or other snacking—intentional or unintentional.
> - Excessive drinking of water can lead to bloat as well. If your dog drinks a lot of water at one time, try having him drink in smaller amounts, not in one huge gulp.
> - Don't overfeed.

© *Margaret H. Bonham*

Deep-chested breeds, such as Labrador Retrievers, are susceptible to bloat.

Chondrodysplasia (CHD)

Chondrodysplasia or "dwarfism" is a genetic disease in certain breeds. Chondrodysplasia causes malformation of the *carpal* and *radius* bones. As a result, the dog's front legs appear stunted and bowed. X-rays up until the age of three months can confirm Chondrodysplasia, but puppies born with this disease do not show outward signs until later. Many veterinarians are not familiar with this disease and may incorrectly classify it as "rickets" or some other nutritional deficiency.

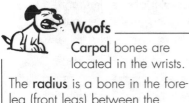

Woofs

Carpal bones are located in the wrists.

The **radius** is a bone in the foreleg (front legs) between the elbow and wrist.

This disease is very painful, and often the only humane choice is to euthanize the dog.

Commonly affected breeds: Alaskan Malamutes, Canadian Inuit Dogs, Beagles.

Elbow Dysplasia (ED)

Elbow dysplasia is a hereditary disease in which the elbow joints are malformed. This disease is called *polygenic* because several genes may cause it.

Surgery, anti-inflammatories, and *nutriceuticals* are recommended treatments for elbow dysplasia. Surgery can be very expensive and arthritis often sets in to the joints, further complicating matters. You should never breed a dog with elbow dysplasia.

Commonly affected breeds: all.

Woofs

A **polygenic** trait or condition comes from more than one gene pair. A **nutriceutical** is a nutritional supplement intended to help mitigate a condition or disease.

© *Margaret H. Bonham*

Always purchase your puppy from a reputable breeder who offers proof that his puppies are screened for genetic diseases.

Entropion and Ectropion

Entropion is a hereditary condition in which the eyelid turns inward into the eye, causing the eyelashes and fur to rub against the eyeball. It is obviously irritating to the dog and usually requires surgery to correct.

Ectropion is where the lower eyelid droops, exposing its interior. In mild cases, your veterinarian may prescribe eye drops and antibiotic and corticosteroid ophthalmic ointment. In severe cases, surgery may be required. Entropion and ectropion are often considered disqualifying faults in the show ring.

Commonly affected breeds: Chow chows, Shar-peis, Pugs, Rottweilers, Cocker Spaniels.

Epilepsy

Epilepsy exists in all breeds and mixed breeds. It is usually hereditary in dogs and quite prevalent in some lines. Studies show some breeds have a genetic predisposition to epilepsy. Idiopathic epilepsy (epilepsy where the specific cause is not known) in dogs is very similar to epilepsy in humans. However, other causes of epilepsy must be ruled out before declaring the condition to be idiopathic. This includes trauma to the head, poisoning, tick paralysis, parasites, deficiencies in certain vitamins, overheating, intestinal obstructions, liver problems, and calcium imbalances.

If your dog is epileptic, your vet will need to perform some tests to rule out other causes. If the seizures are frequent or become worse, your vet usually will prescribe a medication to help control the seizures. You should never breed a dog with epilepsy.

Commonly affected breeds: all. However, Beagles, Siberian Huskies, Cocker Spaniels and all spaniels, and Labrador Retrievers may have a genetic predisposition to it.

© Margaret H. Bonham

Purebred, mixed breed, or hybrid, all dogs are susceptible to genetic and congenital diseases.

Eye Diseases

There are a variety of hereditary and congenital eye diseases in dogs—many that lead to blindness. A veterinary ophthalmologist can determine whether your dog has these or other eye diseases.

The Canine Eye Registry Foundation (CERF) provides a registry for dogs intended for breeding. The CERF evaluation lasts for one year. Any dog you buy should have both its parents registered with CERF. If you plan to breed your dog, you should have his eyes examined and have him registered with CERF.

No Biscuit!

Rage Syndrome, often called *Springer Rage,* is a type of seizure in which the dog becomes suddenly aggressive and bites for no reason. It's called Springer Rage because it appears in Springer Spaniels, but it can appear in any dog. Dogs that have Rage Syndrome are dangerous and there is no cure.

Cataracts

A cataract is a clouding of the eye's lens. The lens may have a small dot or may become opaque, causing complete blindness. Cataracts can stem from either hereditary or environmental causes. Juvenile cataracts are usually hereditary.

Commonly affected breeds: all.

Glaucoma

Glaucoma is a condition in which the body overproduces fluid inside the eyeball and builds up intense pressure. Some forms of glaucoma stem from injury and other conditions, but some forms are inherited. Glaucoma usually requires the removal of the entire eye.

Commonly affected breeds: Siberian Huskies, Beagles, Cocker Spaniels, Basset Hounds.

Hermeralopia (Day Blindness, Cone Degeneration)

Hermeralopia is a hereditary eye condition in which the dog can see well at night, but is blind in daytime or "normal" light conditions. Dogs that suffer from hermeralopia frequently stumble and run into things during the day, but in low light see well and get around with no problems.

Commonly affected breeds: Alaskan Malamutes.

Progressive Retinal Atrophy (PRA) and Central Progressive Retinal Atrophy (CPRA)

PRA and CPRA are two degenerative eye disorders that lead to blindness.

Commonly affected breeds: all.

Hip Dysplasia (HD)

Hip dysplasia is a crippling genetic disease. No amount of good nutrition and care will stop it. It is caused by the malformation of the hip socket. In mildly dysplastic cases, your vet may be able to help mitigate the effects with nutriceuticals such as glucosamine, chondroitin, creatine, and anti-inflammatories such as aspirin. Some cases are so bad that the dog must have surgery. In extreme cases, the dog must be euthanized.

Surgery is expensive, costing thousands of dollars in most cases. This is why it is very important to purchase your purebred from a reputable breeder. You should never breed a dog with hip dysplasia or without an Orthopedic Foundation for Animals (OFA) rating of GOOD or EXCELLENT hips.

Commonly affected breeds: all.

No Biscuit! _____

Hip dysplasia is a devastating disease. Many dogs who have it are in such pain that they need surgery or, in some cases, euthanasia. This is why it is vitally important to have your dog's parents checked for sound hips. Don't take the breeder's word for it; ask for proof. Don't feel embarrassed. Reputable breeders will be happy to show you proof.

Hypothyroidism

The thyroid is an important endocrine gland that secretes hormones that control the body's metabolism at all levels.

Hypothyroidism occurs when the dog's thyroid produces insufficient thyroid hormone. Symptoms can include lethargy, dull and dry coat, obesity or weight gain, and a thinning haircoat. The dog may seek warmer areas. Hypothyroid-ism can cause infertility in intact males and females.

Dog Treats

The OFA, CERF, GDC, and PennHIP all offer various genetic databases for hereditary defects such as hip and elbow dysplasia, eye problems, cardiac problems, thyroid problems, and even epilepsy. If you purchase a puppy, be certain that the breeder shows you proof that your puppy's parents have been screened. See Appendix B.

Some forms of hypothyroidism may be hereditary, so it is inadvisable to breed a hypothyroid dog. Your vet can diagnose hypothyroidism through a blood test. If your dog is hypothyroid, your veterinarian may prescribe a form of thyroid hormone. The OFA has a relatively new thyroid registry. Breeders should test and register their dogs with the OFA.

Commonly affected breeds: all, especially northern breeds such as Siberian Huskies and Alaskan Malamutes, Dobermans, Dachshunds.

Luxating Patella

Luxating Patella is a condition in which the knee slips out of place. Often called "slipped stifle," it can be painful and is only correctible through surgery. It is either a hereditary or congenital condition.

Commonly affected breeds: miniature and toy breeds, Bulldogs.

Osteochondrosis Dissecans (OCD)

Osteochondrosis Dissecans (OCD) is a thickening of the cartilage in joint areas. This thickened cartilage is more prone to damage and may tear and form a flap or rejoin to the bone. OCD may appear in several joints or only one. If your dog has this condition, he may become limp after exercising, suggesting an injury. However, OCD will cause persistent lameness. You may feel the joint pop or crackle as you examine it. Its onset is usually between 4 and 8 months of age.

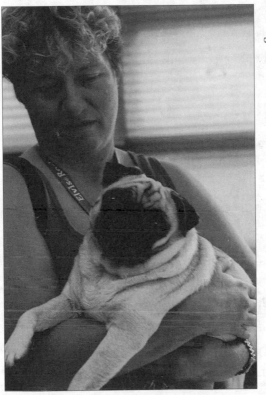

Pugs and other small breeds are susceptible to numerous genetic diseases.

If your dog is diagnosed with OCD, your veterinarian may recommend that you rest him for several weeks. OCD can be very painful, causing a cartilage flap to form over the elbow. That flap may tear or reattach; if the latter happens, surgery is required to remove it.

The Vet Is In

Mixed breed dogs can have genetic diseases, just as their purebred counterparts. The concept of "hybrid vigor" is a bit of a fallacy, because certain genetic diseases such as hip dysplasia are common throughout all the breeds.

OCD can be caused by trauma, although when it is paired with elbow dysplasia it most likely is hereditary.

Commonly affected breeds: all.

Paneosteitis

Paneosteitis or "Pano" is a condition in which a growing puppy suddenly becomes lame. This lameness may be mild to severe and may affect different parts of the puppy at different times. The onset of Pano is somewhere around 5–12 months and usually affects males more than females. Large and giant breeds are usually affected by Pano. It may or may not have a genetic component.

If your puppy has Pano your veterinarian may prescribe analgesics and rest. He may ask you to limit exercise. Eventually, as the puppy gets older, the pain subsides and the puppy grows out of it.

Commonly affected breeds: large and giant breeds.

Protein-Losing Enteropathy (PLE) and Protein-Losing Nephropathy (PLN)

PLE/PLN is a condition wherein either the intestines or the kidneys are unable to process protein correctly and actually lose protein as a result. Unlike Renal Dysplasia (see the following section), PLE/PLN can occur anytime within the dog's life and cannot be reliably screened for until the clinical signs are present. PLE/PLN is a genetic disease, but because the mode of inheritance is unknown, it may have an environmental component. Dogs with PLE or PLN will lose weight, show food allergies, and have diarrhea and vomiting. Veterinarians can diagnose PLE or PLN with a blood chemistry and urine test.

Commonly affected breeds: Soft Coated Wheaten Terriers.

Renal Dysplasia (RD)

Renal Dysplasia or Juvenile Renal Dysplasia is a genetic disease that affects the kidneys. The kidneys are malformed and unable to function properly. Clinical signs of RD usually appear in affected dogs between four months and three years old. Symptoms include excessive thirst and urination and can include vomiting, weight loss, and even diarrhea.

The prognosis is not good for a long life, but your veterinarian can recommend a special low-protein diet and a course of treatment.

Commonly affected breeds: Soft Coated Wheaten Terriers, Golden Retrievers, Norwegian Elkhounds, Lhasa Apsos, Samoyeds, Standard Poodles, Doberman Pinschers, and Cocker Spaniels.

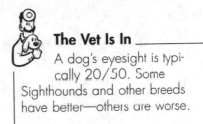

The Vet Is In

A dog's eyesight is typically 20/50. Some Sighthounds and other breeds have better—others are worse.

Aortic Stenosis (AS) and Sub-Aortic Stenosis (SAS)

Aortic Stenosis and Sub-Aortic Stenosis (SAS) is an insidious hereditary condition that may show no outward sign in an apparently healthy dog. The dog may simply drop over dead. AS and SAS is caused by a narrowing of the outflow tract of the left ventricle. In this case, the narrowing occurs below the aortic valve. The heart must work harder to push more blood through the narrow opening, causing more problems.

SAS can be difficult to diagnose. The heart murmur, a common symptom of SAS, may be difficult to detect. The dog may also have arrhythmias. A veterinary cardiologist can diagnose SAS through either Doppler echocardiography or cardiac catheterization. The prognosis for a long healthy life is poor.

Commonly affected breeds: Rottweilers, Newfoundlands, Boxers, German Shepherd Dogs.

Tricuspid Valve Dysplasia (TVD)

Tricuspid Valve Dysplasia (TVD) is a hereditary heart condition. With TVD, the tricuspid valve in the heart is deformed, preventing the valve from closing tightly. The blood leaks from the valve into the right atrium of the heart, causing the right side of the heart to enlarge. TVD can be mild to severe. Puppies with mild TVD can live somewhat normal lives, but puppies with severe TVD will die before they reach one year of age.

The mode of inheritance isn't known yet; researchers continue to look into TVD.

Commonly affected breeds: Labrador Retrievers.

Von Willebrand's Disease (VWD)

Von Willebrand's Disease (VWD) is a type of hemophilia (uncontrollable bleeding) in dogs. There are various levels of hemophilia—some dogs have it more severely than others. There are two types of Von Willebrand's Disease: inherited and acquired. The acquired form of Von Willebrand's is associated with familial autoimmune thyroid disease. Your veterinarian can diagnose VWD through a blood test.

Dogs with VWD are susceptible to uncontrollable bleeding. If your dog has VWD, your veterinarian should take precautions during surgery to prevent the dog from bleeding out. Likewise, you should take precautions to avoid the chance of injuring your dog if he has VWD.

Commonly affected breeds: terriers (all), Doberman Pinschers, Golden Retrievers, Rottweilers, Weimaraners, Standard Poodles.

Zinc Responsive Dermatosis

In zinc responsive dermatosis, the dog's body fails to absorb enough zinc from the dog's food, even if the diet has adequate amounts. This disease usually has a genetic component, so dogs displaying clear signs of zinc responsive dermatosis should not be bred.

The symptoms include scaly nose, paw pads, and belly. It may be confused with pemphigus or "collie nose." Treatment of zinc responsive dermatosis requires additional zinc supplementation to the dog's diet.

Commonly affected breeds: northern breeds (such as Alaskan Malamutes, Samoyeds, and Siberians Huskies).

There are many more congenital and hereditary diseases among dogs. Some breeds are more predisposed to certain diseases than others. Contact the national breed club for your breed for a list of potential genetic diseases.

The Vet Is In _____

Sled dogs—Alaskan Huskies, Alaskan Malamutes, Siberian Huskies, and Samoyeds—have a higher incidence of zinc responsive dermatosis than other breeds.

© *Margaret H. Bonham*

Malamutes and other northern breeds can suffer from Chondrodysplasia, zinc responsive dermatosis, and other hereditary and congenital diseases.

The Least You Need to Know

- All breeds and mixed breeds are susceptible to both hereditary and congenital conditions.

- Bloat is a life-threatening condition where the dog's stomach fills with gas and fluid. Seek immediate veterinary attention for bloat.

- Elbow dysplasia can be a painful hereditary disease in dogs and may require surgery.

- Eye diseases such as PRA are common in dogs.

- Hip Dysplasia is a devastating hereditary disease prevalent in dogs. No amount of nutrition or medication can prevent Hip Dysplasia. Surgery for Hip Dysplasia may run into thousands of dollars.

Chapter 12

The Golden Years

In This Chapter

- 🏠 Learn how to keep your dog active and healthy for a long life
- 🏠 Understand how to keep your older dog comfortable despite arthritis and other signs of aging
- 🏠 Should you get a new puppy as your other dog ages?
- 🏠 How to handle euthanasia and grief

Someday, you'll notice that your dog is graying around the muzzle, or perhaps he's a little stiff when he gets up in the morning. Someday, you'll wake up and your dog will be old.

This isn't a time for sadness; it's a time to enjoy each other. Dogs can and do live healthy and physically active lives beyond the age of 10. It's very possible—I've had several dogs who have lived to 14 or 15 years old. Part of the credit for longevity is due to genetics, but part is also due to medical care, diet, and physical activity. You can't change genetics, but you can make a crucial difference in your dog's health and longevity.

In this chapter, I focus on the older dog. Yes, he's more susceptible to cancers and tumors, but he's also more fun to be around.

Gone are the fun but sometimes trying puppy days; now you can enjoy your mature best friend. I'll cover how to make your dog more comfortable and whether you should bring a new dog in at this time. I'll also cover the eventuality of euthanasia and how to know when it's your dog's time.

Having an Active Mind and Active Body Means a Healthy, Long Life

When does the term "old" begin to apply for a dog? It depends. Just as some people don't seem old even when they're in their 70s, some dogs don't seem old when others do. Good genetics and a lifetime of exercise, good nutrition, and medical care can make the difference.

The Vet Is In

Some dogs are "seniors" at seven years or greater. This is especially true with the giant breeds such as the Great Dane. But some dogs can live beyond 15 years with good care. From 8 to 10 years old, your dog will start showing more changes due to old age. After 10, I would start calling the dog a senior.

Senior Activities

Just because your dog is old doesn't mean he's ready for the rocking chair on the porch. If your dog has been healthy and active, there's no reason he shouldn't continue being healthy and active. In fact, if you start taking away his activities, you may find that he'll start deteriorating faster.

Keep an eye on your dog when you work or exercise him. He may not be able to do everything a younger dog can, so don't insist on the same physical abilities of a younger dog. But don't retire him yet, either, unless he has a medical problem or injury that precludes the activity. Some older dogs enjoy a scaled-down version of the activity—it allows them to have fun and interact with you.

Feeding the Older Dog

Feed your dog according to his weight and activity level. Don't necessarily switch him over to a "senior" diet unless he's gaining weight, his activity level has decreased, or he has a physical condition that warrants a change in dog food. Many of my "senior" dogs still work and are active—and get premium performance dog food.

Some vets recommend lowering the protein in a senior dog's diet to avoid stressing the kidneys, but the jury is still out on that. If your dog is still working and does not suffer from kidney disease, don't lower the protein—he still needs it for repairing his muscles. Some studies on kidney disease suggest reducing protein levels is beneficial, while others show that a dog with kidney disease might benefit from protein.

No Biscuit!

Older dogs are more prone to tumors and cancers. Examine your dog for tumors; if you find one, take him to the vet. Cancer is a little harder to diagnose without running tests. If your dog is eating but losing weight, drinking excessive water, tiring easily, or not eating well at all, take him to the vet for a full examination.

Keeping Your Old Dog Comfortable

Older dogs tend to enjoy a nice warm bed. Dogs who formerly eschewed the comforts of home tend to enjoy them now. A soft bed made from orthopedic foam can help relieve pressure points. Some pet equipment manufacturers have developed electric heating mats that radiate constant warmth for the dog. If you use one of these, be certain that the cord is hidden so that your dog can't chew it and accidentally shock himself.

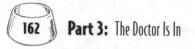

The stairs that were once an obstacle only when your dog was a small puppy now may become a real problem. If you can, move his crate or bed to the lower part of the house so that he doesn't have to climb stairs anymore. Or perhaps install a ramp.

 No Biscuit!

Never give analgesics such as acetaminophen or ibuprofen to your dog. These are very poisonous to dogs. Talk to your vet about anti-inflammatories and the proper dosages.

As your dog gets older, he may have trouble chewing his food. Moistening his dog food or feeding him canned food is an alternative that will help make your dog more comfortable.

Getting Old

Dogs experience more problems as they age, including loss of certain senses, cancers and tumors, and, of course, arthritis. Many problems can be mitigated with modern veterinary medicine, but vets aren't miracle workers. If you notice that your dog has a particular problem, it's best to take him to the vet right away, rather than wait for it to become a bigger problem.

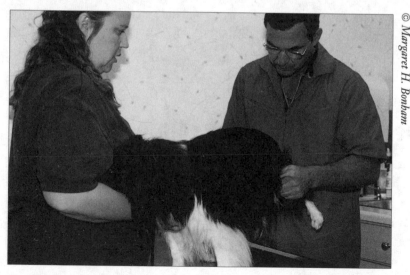

© Margaret H. Bonham

Dr. Wingert checks a Sheltie for arthritis.

Arthritis

Arthritis seems a constant in age—for both people and dogs. If your dog is not active, you may see signs of arthritis early. Some supplements, such as glucosamine and MSM (found in Cosequin, Glycoflex, or Synova-Cre), can help relieve arthritis. These supplements work well on some dogs and do nothing for others. Your dog usually has to be on it for over six weeks before you can see any effect.

Your vet can help mitigate some of the effects of arthritis with anti-inflammatories. Aspirin is a common pain reliever—ask your vet for the proper dosage. Do not give your dog either acetaminophen or ibuprofen—they are very poisonous to dogs. Your vet can prescribe the right amount of buffered aspirin, anti-inflammatories, or steroids to alleviate pain and swelling.

Blindness

You may not even notice if your dog goes blind. Most dogs are quite adept at getting around their home and even their neighborhood even though they're blind. The owner usually notices something is amiss when the dog bumps into something that normally isn't there. Have your vet confirm your suspicions if you think your dog is blind.

Now is not the time to rearrange the furniture. Keep your dog at home and in familiar surroundings if he is blind or impaired visually. Don't let him off the leash or he might wander around and become lost. When in a strange place, keep him beside you—you are his seeing-eye person now!

But your dog doesn't necessarily have to go blind or remain without sight. Depending on the type of eye problem he has, veterinary advances may help restore his sight. Vet ophthalmologists can diagnose and treat certain problems such as cataracts and glaucoma. Corneal transplants—once possible only in the realm of human medicine—are available to dogs as well.

Cancer and Tumors

Cancer and tumors become more prevalent with age. Some cancers and tumors can be eliminated or greatly reduced if you spay or neuter your dog before six months.

If you find a lump or bump that isn't normally on your dog, have it checked immediately. Some cancers and tumors are fast-spreading; if you wait too long, it may be too late for your veterinarian to do anything about them. Signs of cancer include strange growths, excessive weight loss, lack of appetite, bleeding, sores or wounds that will not heal, abnormal swellings, excessive sleep or lethargy, and difficulty breathing, eating, or drinking.

Treatment for cancer or tumors is similar to treatment of cancer and tumors in humans. This includes surgery, chemotherapy, and radiation therapy. There are newer, experimental treatments for cancer, including gene therapy, but they can be very costly.

 No Biscuit! _____

One controversial medication commonly prescribed for arthritis is Rimadyl™—also known as Carprofen. Some dogs have developed liver disease while on Rimadyl. Still, many vets prescribe Rimadyl to help alleviate arthritis pain.

I've had an older dog on Rimadyl with no apparent side effects. If your dog is suffering from arthritis and you wish to try Rimadyl, talk to your vet about potential risks and side effects. Your vet may wish to run blood tests to determine if your dog is right for Rimadyl.

Cognitive Dysfunction Syndrome (CDS)

Cognitive Dysfunction Syndrome is similar to Alzheimer's disease in dogs. This disease is marked by an abrupt change in behavior. Your dog may suddenly look "lost" in the room. He may not recognize loved ones and may forget his housebreaking. His sleep may be disrupted and he may bark and carry on in the middle of the night.

Brain tumors may mimic CDS, so it is very important to have a brain tumor ruled out before putting your dog through CDS treatment. The CDS treatment of choice is Anipryl, which is also used to treat Cushing's Disease (a disease of the pituitary or adrenal glands) in dogs. The therapy can be expensive, costing $50 to $100 a month. Once the dog is on the therapy, he must remain on it his entire life or symptoms will reappear.

Congestive Heart Failure

Your dog may have congestive heart failure if he coughs or has respiratory distress, fluid buildup in the limbs, and tires easily after even light exercise. There's no cure and it will ultimately be fatal, but it can be mitigated by diet and medication. You can help prevent congestive heart failure by keeping your dog active and fit. Obesity can help cause or aggravate congestive heart failure. Low-salt diets can benefit dogs with congestive heart failure. Consult your vet about diets with low salt.

Deafness

If your dog acts as if he's ignoring you, he may be going deaf. Deafness can come on gradually or suddenly. Clap your hands behind your dog's head or rattle the food bowl while he's in the other room. If he doesn't react, he's probably deaf.

Deaf dogs can be exceedingly frustrating. You'll find yourself shouting at the dog for no good reason—as though your dog will hear you if you talk louder. The truth is that once the hearing goes, your dog is unlikely to hear even shouting. Some deaf dogs can hear whistles, but many hear nothing at all.

The Vet Is In

Hearing aids for dogs? That's right—you can get hearing aids for your dog. These hearing aids are specially made for the dog and may offer a quality of life that the dog wouldn't have without them.

If your dog is deaf, you'll have to teach him hand signals. We have one deaf dog in the house. When we first started trying to teach him hand signals, it looked like a mime locked in the room with an angry bee. Start slowly—teach your dog as you would a puppy. It may take a little bit of time for him to pick up on it, but most dogs are pretty clever and figure out what we want in spite of ourselves.

Dental Problems

Older dogs are more prone to dental problems due to worn or chipped teeth and tartar buildup. Stinky breath, bleeding gums, loss of appetite, broken teeth, or a buildup of brown tartar or plaque indicates the need to go to the vet for a tooth cleaning and possible extraction.

You can keep your dog's teeth healthy by brushing them often and giving him chews that help clean his teeth and gums.

Urinary Tract Problems

Signs of bladder or kidney problems include bloody or dark urine, frequency in drinking and urination, hunched up back, and pain while urinating.

If your dog shows blood in his urine or if he acts as though it is difficult to urinate, you should bring him to your vet for an examination. Dogs, like people, can get kidney stones and bladder stones. If your dog has either, depending on his condition, your vet may prescribe a urine acidifier and antibiotics or may have to operate.

Hard water, forcing a dog to "hold it" for long hours, and diet may contribute to urinary tract problems.

Should You Get a Second Dog?

Some people decide to get a puppy as their dog ages. The idea is to help mitigate the pain of losing the beloved pet when the time finally arrives. This can be good or bad, depending on the circumstances. If your dog is very old, he may look on this new puppy as an interloper. A puppy will take most of your time and energy—leaving little time for your older dog. Your dog may feel neglected and may become aggressive or short-tempered with your new pup.

However, some dogs tolerate puppies well. Sometimes a puppy can spark new life into an older dog. Something new and exciting can shake an older dog from the routine enough to make him feel young again. Some older dogs are quick to become the puppy's aunt or uncle, and are delighted to "show the ropes" to the newcomer.

Dog Treats

If you decide to bring another dog or a puppy into the family, always choose a neutral area such as a park for the dogs to meet. Let your dog greet the newcomer while on the leash. Praise your dog for good behavior and discourage bad behavior. It may take a few sessions before you can let your dog loose with the other dog or puppy.

Whether another dog or puppy is accepted largely depends on you and your dog. If your dog gets along with other dogs and puppies, perhaps getting a puppy is the right choice. At the same time, you must take the time to make your dog feel extra special. Don't stop doing things with her now that you have the puppy—otherwise she will associate the lack of attention with the appearance of the interloper.

Identifying Serious Medical Conditions

Hopefully, your dog will have a long and healthy life, free from any serious medical conditions. But, as your dog gets older, you may become good friends with your vet—and not by choice. As dogs get older, like people, they suffer from a number of ailments. Some may be serious or debilitating. You may have some tough choices ahead.

When faced with any medical dilemma, the first thing to think about is the quality of your dog's life. Will the treatment enhance his quality of life? Are you taking a risk having an already debilitated dog go through treatment or surgery? These are questions only you and your vet can answer.

Remember that your dog has no idea that what he is going through will help him. All he knows is that he is suffering. When you choose a treatment, consider what your dog is going through. Talk to your vet about proper pain management and about what will improve the quality of life for your pet.

Saying Good-Bye

Saying good-bye is perhaps the hardest thing to do as a dog owner. I've had to put several of my dogs down and the truth is, it doesn't get any easier. Nor is the decision always clear-cut.

Sometimes it's obvious: Your dog is in great pain and is dying from a terminal disease or injury. Other times, the diagnosis is unclear, or you're sitting in an emergency room and don't know what to do. Heroic efforts may be required to save him, which cost far beyond what you can afford; and your dog might have a very slim chance of recovery anyway. In times like this, talk to someone you can trust—perhaps your own vet, or you might obtain a second opinion. Other friends who are dog owners may be able to see clearly when you cannot. They may offer you advice untainted by the emotions of the situation.

Putting an End to the Suffering

Don't allow your best friend to suffer needlessly. While it is tempting to try heroic actions to save your pet, you may discover that the result is still the same. Dogs don't live forever, and even though you want your dog to live a little longer, it may not be humane or within anyone's capability.

Euthanasia is painless and quick. The veterinarian administers an injection and your pet peacefully goes to sleep. You can stay with your dog during his final minutes, or leave—your choice. Many pet owners opt to stay with their dog during the last few minutes because it brings closure.

Grieving

Grieving is normal and natural. Don't talk to non–dog owners about it, because they will be the most callous. They may tell you it was only a pet. No, it wasn't. Your dog was your friend and it would be callous to not grieve for a good friend who just died.

Talk to your vet about grief. He or she may be able to refer you to free or low-cost pet loss counseling. Many veterinary colleges or humane societies offer free or low-cost pet loss hotlines. Take care of yourself during this time. Keep busy and active—exercise and eat a balanced diet. Avoid being alone and going into depression. You aren't denying that you have grief over the loss—you are helping yourself deal with it.

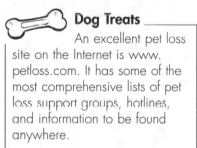 **Dog Treats**
An excellent pet loss site on the Internet is www. petloss.com. It has some of the most comprehensive lists of pet loss support groups, hotlines, and information to be found anywhere.

With time, the pain and anguish of your pet's death will fade. You will start remembering all the good times you had together. Perhaps, in time, you'll be ready to own another dog again. Perhaps you will get a puppy to keep you occupied. If you do, remember that no puppy will replace your beloved pet and that no dog will be like your dog. Your new puppy or dog will have a different personality and different behaviors—don't expect the same thing out of this puppy. However, in time, you may grow to love this new addition as much as your beloved pet.

The Least You Need to Know

- Keeping your older dog active will help him lead a longer, better life.

- Your older dog will need your help coping with arthritis, blindness, deafness, and other old-age illnesses.

- Carefully consider getting a new puppy as your dog ages.

- You will grieve when your dog dies. Don't let him suffer needlessly just to postpone the inevitable.

Part 4

Dinnertime!

"What's for dinner?" That's the first thing on your dog's mind. Good nutrition is very important for your dog's health. But what is best to feed your dog? Should you cook his meals? Feed a raw diet? Or should you go with commercial food? And if so, which one?

In Part 4, we cover commercial dog food. What's out there and what's available. What AAFCO stands for and what it means when the food is formulated in accordance to AAFCO guidelines.

You'll learn the importance of protein, fats, and carbohydrates in a dog's diet. You'll learn what vitamins and minerals do and whether it's a good idea to supplement or not. Last, you'll be able to make sense of the mumbo jumbo that's on a dog food label.

Chapter 13

The Lowdown on Commercial Dog Food

In This Chapter

- 🏠 Evaluating premium dog foods versus bargain brand dog foods
- 🏠 Choosing the right dog food
- 🏠 Comparing types of dog foods
- 🏠 Dispelling myths about feeding your dog

Your dog's nutrition plays a critical role in his health, but what should you feed your dog? You've no doubt heard various opinions on what is right to feed him.

In this chapter, I'll discuss commercial dog foods and premium versus bargain brands—is there a difference? Also, what type of dog food is best for your dog—dry, canned, frozen, semisoft, or meat rolls?

I also discuss common dog food fallacies and myths associated with feeding. You'll be surprised to learn that some things you've heard over the years might not be just wrong, but downright dangerous.

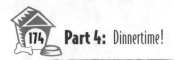
Deciding If You Should Feed a Commercial Dog Food

Dog food today benefits from research done in feeding trials and with canine athletes such as sled dogs. We know more about dog nutrition than we did 20 years ago.

© *Margaret H. Bonham*

The dog food you feed should be a premium brand that is easy to find, has a high digestibility percentage, and is palatable. All that good nutrition does no good if your dog won't eat it!

That bag of premium dog food in your pantry is the culmination of intensive research and testing. Most premium dog food companies strictly adhere to, if not try to surpass, the AAFCO guidelines for dog nutrition. Formulating a dog food is a careful balancing act—one that requires in-depth knowledge of phosphorus/calcium ratios, fat, protein and carbohydrate percentages, and trace mineral supplementation.

> **Dog Treats**
> Always look on the label of a dog food to be certain it meets or exceeds AAFCO (American Association of Feed Control Officials) guidelines.

Still, some people aren't convinced. They think they can concoct a better formula than veterinarians and nutritionists. In some cases, perhaps they have. But how close do you think they can come to formulating a complete and balanced dog food at home? It can be done, but it is very difficult.

> **No Biscuit!**
>
> Certain foods should never be fed to dogs. These include:
>
> 🐾 **Chocolate.** Contains a poisonous substance called theobromine that can make a dog very sick or even kill him. Dark (bittersweet or baker's) chocolate is more poisonous than milk chocolate.
>
> 🐾 **Onions.** Can cause anemia.
>
> 🐾 **Raw salmon from the Northwest.** Contains a parasite that can kill your dog.
>
> 🐾 **Alcohol.** Even a small amount can cause alcohol poisoning. A drunk dog is *not* funny and a small amount can be extremely toxic.

If you want to provide your dog a homemade diet, there are many good books available to help you. But be careful! Many diets are improperly balanced, and can cause severe nutritional deficiencies. When in doubt, consult your veterinarian or talk to a nutritionist at a veterinary college. (See Chapter 19 for more on homemade diets.)

Determining Premium vs. Bargain Brand

Is there a difference in a premium brand versus a bargain brand? In a word, yes.

It's tempting to go with the bag of $10 dog food when you see the premium dog food costs $30 to $40 a bag. After all, dog food is dog food, isn't it? A quick look at the guaranteed analysis shows that the food has 22 percent protein and 10 percent fat—well within AAFCO norms. Certainly all dog food is the same, isn't it?

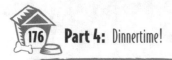

Actually, no. The difference between a premium and bargain brand is more than just price. It's the quality of the ingredients. Premium dog food usually uses ingredients that are more digestible and has a greater nutrient value than the bargain brands. That means that you feed less and you have less to scoop up in your backyard when your dog poops.

Many bargain brands use cheaper ingredients such as soy protein, meat and bone meal, and fillers. These ingredients add bulk to the dog food, so you must feed more to obtain the correct amount of nutrition. They often have cute shapes, colors, and artificial flavors to enhance the palatability. Your dog doesn't need this and neither does your pocketbook. Some bargain brands require that you feed twice or more the amount of food you would with a premium diet. The savings you make by buying a cheaper food literally gets eaten up by your dog because you must feed more.

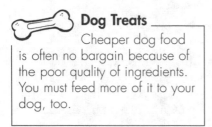

Dog Treats

Cheaper dog food is often no bargain because of the poor quality of ingredients. You must feed more of it to your dog, too.

© *Margaret H. Bonham*

Puppies have different nutritional needs than adults. These two Samoyed pups need all the energy of a premium puppy food.

Choosing a Commercial Dog Food

There are a bewildering number of premium dog foods out there. How do you choose the right one for your dog? If you've purchased a puppy from a breeder, the breeder may already have been feeding a perfectly acceptable dog food.

First, consider the age of your dog. Is he a puppy or adult? Puppies require growth formula until they're a year old or more. If your dog is an adult, you have several choices. Is he active or a couch potato? Does he work as a sled dog or hunting dog or is he a little too pudgy? All these variables should factor in when selecting a dog food. (See Chapter 20 for more info on puppy food and adult dog food.)

Besides these factors you should also take into account the availability, the quality, and the palatability of the dog food.

Availability

The dog food you choose should be from a recognizable dog food manufacturer. It should be readily available at several locations so that if Chez Haute Pet Boutique is out or doesn't carry it anymore, you can purchase the dog food somewhere else close by. You don't need to be searching halfway across town for your dog's food.

Quality

The quality of the dog food is equally important. The first ingredient should be a protein source, such as chicken, beef, by-products, or meat meal. Avoid dog foods with soy or meat and bone meal as the first protein source, as both soy and bone meal are not as high quality and generally not as digestible as meat or by-products.

The dog food should have a high *digestibility* content. This means that the dog should metabolize more of the food instead

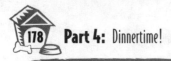
of it going out the other end. Premium dog foods generally have 80 percent or better digestibility and super-premium dog foods are 90 percent or more. You can obtain digestibility percentages by contacting the dog food manufacturer directly.

Woofs

Digestibility is the percentage of the dog's food that he metabolizes rather than eliminates.

Whatever dog food you choose, check the label to be certain it meets or exceeds AAFCO guidelines.

Palatability

All the nutrition in the world isn't any good if your dog won't eat it. Some dogs snub certain premium dog foods only to wolf down cheap brands because of the high salt, flavorings, and sugar content.

Some pet food manufacturers have sample packets available at feed stores or dog shows. Get a few sample packets and try them out or buy the smallest bag possible. Canned, frozen, and beef rolls are highly palatable and most dogs will eat these readily or will eat them when they are mixed with dry dog food.

Evening It Up: Figuring Out the Nutrition Content on a Caloric Basis

The Guaranteed Analysis on a dog food label varies greatly according to type of food. Canned dog food would *appear* to have less nutrition than dry dog food, but this is because the Guaranteed Analysis is done by weight, not through caloric percentages. (Chapter 14 shows how to calculate true dry-matter content.)

When you calculate the dog food's nutrition based on caloric percentages, you can "even it up" and be able to compare the food on a caloric or energy basis.

How do you determine calories and percentage of calories in dog foods? If you look at the Guaranteed Analysis on a dog food label, you will see something that looks like the following:

Guaranteed Analysis

Crude protein not less than 26 percent

Crude fat not less than 15 percent

Crude fiber not more than 3 percent

Moisture not more than 11 percent

Ash not more than 6 percent

On this imaginary label, you can see that protein makes up 26 percent *by weight*. This means that 26 percent of the weight is in the form of crude protein. If you add up all the numbers, you will find that all these numbers add up to 61 percent. The other 39 percent of the dry matter is carbohydrates. Protein and carbohydrates are 4 kilocalories per gram. Fat is 9 kilocalories per gram. To calculate the percentage of nutrient's calories per 100 grams, take the percentage and multiply it by the kilocalories per gram. For example: Protein is 26 percent or 26 gm/100 gm. Multiply 26 gm/100 gm by 4 Kcal/gm to get 104 Kcals per 100 gm. Do the same for the carbohydrates and fat. Add the caloric values for protein, carbohydrates, and fat to get the total calories per 100 gm.

Protein = 26 gm/100 gm × 4 Kcal/gm = 104 Kcal/100 gm

Carbohydrates = 39 gm/100 gm × 4 Kcal/gm = 156 Kcal/100 gm

Fat = 15 gm/100 gm × 9 Kcal/gm = 135 Kcal/100 gm

395 Kcals/100 gm

To determine what percentage is protein, fat, and carbohydrates, divide the respective nutrient's calories by the total number of calories to get a percentage. As you can see from the example, fat makes up 34 percent of the calories and carbohydrates make up 39 percent.

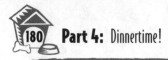

If you add the percentages together, you will have 99 percent. (The 1 percent was lost in rounding error.)

104 ÷ 395 = 26 percent protein

156 ÷ 395 = 39 percent carbohydrates

135 ÷ 395 = 34 percent fat

Now, let's consider an imaginary high performance dog food:

Guaranteed Analysis

Crude protein not less than 30 percent

Crude fat not less than 20 percent

Crude fiber not more than 3 percent

Moisture not more than 11 percent

Ash not more than 6 percent

This dog food would calculate out to 29 percent protein, 43 percent fat, and 29 percent carbohydrates, using the above formula.

Making Decisions: Types of Dog Food Available

What form of food should you feed your dog—dry, canned, semi-moist, frozen, freeze-dried, or compressed? Each has its advantages and disadvantages.

I feed my dogs dry dog food because of the cost-effectiveness and the variety. Because I have a large number of dogs, it doesn't make sense for me to feed other types of food. At the same time, I make certain that the dog food has the nutrition that my dogs

> **Dog Treats**
> Choose a dog food that is readily available in your town so that if one store stops carrying it, you can find it in another store.

require, whether they're backpacking, running in a sled team, running an agility course, or lying around the house.

Occasionally, if I have a sick dog or a dog under stress, I may feed canned dog food for increased palatability. Because I race sled dogs, my dogs have different nutritional requirements than pets or even very active dogs, so I supplement. (See Chapter 20 about sled dog diets for more information.)

© *Margaret H. Bonham*

Wolves don't hunt tofu in the wild—nor do they eat strictly muscle meat. Don't feed your dog a vegetarian or all-meat diet or you run the risk of causing serious deficiencies. Feed your dog a good-quality, premium dog food with a meat base.

Dry Dog Food

Pound for pound, dry dog food or kibble is the most cost-effective dog food. You have more choices in dry dog food than other forms. Some manufacturers only offer dog food in kibble form. It's easy to store, has a shelf life between six months to one year, and is easy to feed. Dry food is best to keep teeth clean. The downside to kibble is that some dogs can be picky with it.

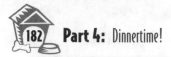

Canned Dog Food

Canned dog food is probably the second most available food. It's extremely palatable, and has a good shelf life (one to three years), but can be expensive, costing anywhere from 50¢ to $2.00 a can. You're paying mostly for water and processing. Dogs that eat canned food may need more frequent dental cleanings than dogs that eat kibble.

Preparing canned food is slightly more difficult than dry dog food—you need a can opener and a spoon. Canned food will spoil rapidly once opened, so unused portions must go into the fridge and stink up your fridge. (Helpful hint: Don't put it next to the Sunday roast.) Most dog owners who use canned food mix it with the dog's dry food for enhanced palatability.

> **Dog Treats**
> Many dog owners like to feed dry food and then mix another type of food in for palatability or as a treat.

Semimoist Dog Food

Semimoist food comes in the shape of hamburger patties. It's chock full of colors, sugar (corn syrup to maintain that semisoftness), salt, and preservatives. It's expensive too. Not recommended as a daily food.

Frozen Dog Food

This is a relatively new type of dog food. Mostly meat, it can be expensive, costing $1 to $3 a pound. Like canned food, you're paying for water, but unlike canned food, you're also paying for storage. This type of dog food is extremely palatable, but it isn't as available as dry or canned food. (Stores need freezer space for the food.) If your dog is big, storage for frozen food can become a problem, unless you have a large freezer. (Don't mistake it for the Sunday roast!) Frozen dog food is highly perishable and must be kept frozen until used. It is not as readily available as dry and canned food and preparation is more complicated than dry. (You must either thaw the food or slice off portions.)

Freeze-Dried Dog Food

Another new type of dog food, this is the equivalent of frozen dog food with the water removed. It is very expensive—8 pounds may cost over $50—but you re-hydrate and feed less. The shelf life is very good—equivalent to dry dog food in most cases. Palatability is good as well, but it is not available in all areas. It's fairly easy to feed, but you should add water to the food.

Compressed Dog Food Rolls

Compressed dog food rolls are a relatively new dog food phenomenon as well. They're soft and have some moisture, but are compact. Highly palatable, most dogs like the smell and taste. They're expensive when compared to dry food, costing $10 to $15 for a 2 to 5 pound roll. Once opened, they must be stored in the refrigerator. To feed, you must slice off portions of the food. Shelf life is typically less than dry food and availability is better than frozen or dehydrated food, but less than dry or canned.

> **No Biscuit!**
> Dog food doesn't last forever, despite the preservatives. Most dry dog food has a shelf life of six months to one year. Feeding rancid dog food can cause your dog to become sick. When in doubt, toss it out!

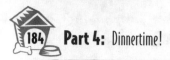

The Least You Need to Know

- Poisonous foods for dogs include chocolate, raw salmon from the Northwest, onions, and alcohol.

- Not all dog foods are the same. Bargain brands tend to be no bargain because they have more fillers and are less digestible than premium brands.

- The dog food you choose should be palatable to your dog, have a high-quality meat source as the first ingredient, and have over 80 percent digestibility.

- When choosing a dog food, choose a premium brand that is easy for you to find in case the store you buy it at runs out.

- Feed a dog food that meets or exceeds AAFCO standards.

- Dog food can take various forms. The most cost-effective and the easiest to store and prepare is dry dog food.

Chapter 14

A Dog Food by Any Other Name ...

In This Chapter

-  Feeding schedules
- Knowing how much food should you feed
- Choosing healthy snacks
- Determining if table scraps and junk food are okay
- Changing dog foods without upsetting your dog's stomach

You've selected the right dog food. How much do you feed him? And how often? Not all dog food contains the right caloric value, and the feeding guidelines aren't always appropriate.

In this chapter, I discuss how much and how often you should feed your dog. Should you add table scraps? Which snacks are healthy and which ones aren't? I also include a few recipes for fun snacks to make on your own.

© *Margaret H. Bonham*

Feed your adult dog twice daily.

How Much? How Often? Feeding Schedules

I swear that my dogs have wristwatches. At 6 o'clock, they start nagging me for dinner. Actually, it starts well before 6 P.M.—sometimes as early as an hour before. Dogs are very observant and if you've ever owned one, this is an all too familiar scenario.

But how often should you feed your dog? I've seen feeding schedules of all sorts, but as a rule, you should feed puppies younger than six months three times a day. Adult dogs can eat twice a day.

> ![bone] **Dog Treats**
> Check the dog food package for feeding guidelines. Most feeding guidelines on a package suggest too much food, but it's a place to start when feeding your dog.

Puppies need to eat more often for two reasons. The first is they need extra nutrition because they are growing. The second is their stomachs are smaller and can't consume their daily amount in just one sitting. Because their stomachs are smaller, they need smaller portions, but still must eat enough to grow.

© Margaret H. Bonham

Puppies younger than six months should be fed three times a day.

How much dog food you should feed is the subject of much debate. Look at the feeding guidelines on the package. Most guidelines tend to overfeed to prevent you from feeding your dog too little. Try the amount suggested and then increase or reduce the amount fed according to your dog's age, weight, fitness, and activity level. If the guidelines are intended for the amount in one day, split the food into two or three equal portions depending on whether you feed two or three times a day.

Establish times to feed your dog. Fix his meal and set it down. If he doesn't eat in 10 minutes, pick up his food and let him wait it out until the next mealtime. Don't feel sorry for him or give him treats—you're trying to teach him to be a good eater.

Should I Free Feed?

Free feeding means leaving the food out for the dog to consume when he wants to. It might seem a good idea because you don't have to hassle with a mealtime, you just dump the dog food in a bowl and leave it out all day.

Woofs

Free feeding is the practice of leaving your dog's food out all day so he can eat as he chooses.

Free feeding isn't a good idea, however. For one thing, you can't monitor how much your dog has eaten. Dogs are like people—some have willpower to keep fit, but many don't and will overeat. Some breeds are such chow hounds that they'll inhale just about everything set in front of them.

Dog Treats

The following is a nifty dog biscuit recipe. Not to AAFCO guidelines, certainly, but a fun treat you can bake for your dog.

Microwave Dog Biscuits

$^1/_2$ cup all-purpose flour
$^3/_4$ cup non-fat dry milk powder
$^1/_2$ cup quick-cooking rolled oats
$^1/_4$ cup yellow cornmeal
1 tsp. sugar
$^1/_3$ cup shortening
1 egg, slightly beaten
1 TB. instant bouillon granules—either beef or chicken
$^1/_2$ cup hot water

Combine flour, milk powder, rolled oats, cornmeal, and sugar in medium bowl. Cut in shortening until mixture resembles coarse crumbs. Add egg to this dry mixture, and stir. Add bouillon into hot water until dissolved. Slowly pour hot water/bouillon into flour mixture and blend with a fork until all is moistened. Form dough into a ball and knead on floured board 5 minutes, or until smooth and elastic. Divide dough in half and roll out each half to about $^1/_2$ inch thick. Make cut-outs with cookie cutters, or make nuggets by rolling round into 1-inch diameter log, and cutting into $^1/_2$ inch pieces. Arrange six cut-out shapes or 24 nuggets on a 10-inch plate. Microwave at 50 percent (medium) for 5 to 10 minutes, or until firm and dry to the touch. Rotate plate every 2 minutes and turn shapes over half way through the cooking time. Cool on wire rack. Shapes will crisp as they cool.

Courtesy of *Canine Classified*, Anne Page, reprinted with permission.

There are other good reasons not to free feed. One is if your dog misses a meal, you'll be sure to catch it. It's not "normal" for dogs to skip meals—it's a sign of a health problem. If your dog is normally a good eater, you'll be able to catch a health problem if he suddenly turns up his nose at his food.

From a training standpoint, free feeding is a bad idea. The dog food magically appears every day without your dog making the association that it comes from you. Because you should be the pur-veyor of all good things, doesn't it make sense that your dog associates food with you?

No Biscuit!

If your dog skips a meal, it may be a sign that he isn't feeling well, especially if he is a good eater. A trip to the vet might be in order.

What About Snack Time?

Limit your dog's treats to no more than 10 percent of his normal diet. When you do give treats they should hopefully be nutritious. Many treats shaped like human food have artificial colors, salt, preservatives, and sugar to entice both the owner and the dog. Use these sparingly, as most are very high in calories. A good puppy or adult biscuit by a premium dog food manufacturer is preferable to these as they are nutritionally balanced and aren't as fattening.

I like to give my dogs crunchy biscuits. Mother Hubbard makes a really good biscuit in different flavors, but there are others equally good for your dog.

I've included a few fun treats in this chapter that you can try out. I'm convinced that the dogs love these homemade goodies more because they've seen you slave over a hot stove (or microwave, in one case) to produce them. A few miscreants will turn up their noses at them (I had one dog that turned up baked liver treats!), but most will appreciate your efforts. At the very least, they are okay for humans, so if your dog doesn't like them, maybe you will.

Why Not Junk Food or Table Scraps?

Of course, there are those who have convinced themselves that it is tantamount to animal cruelty to not share your supper with your dog. You know who you are. There are 12-step programs out there.

The truth is that if you do this, you're teaching your dog bad habits by feeding him people food. You're teaching him to beg with those adorable soul-searching eyes, and you're teaching him to be a picky eater. Does your dog eat his regular food without "a little something"? Does he mug you for your food when you sit down to dinner? Have you had a roast stolen off the counter or your plate licked clean?

> **No Biscuit!**
> Table scraps and other "junk foods" are high in fat, carbohydrates, sugar, and salt. If you must feed it, keep the portions small and less than 5 percent of your dog's diet.

Could there be a possible connection? Hmmmmm …

Besides the bad habits, you're causing an imbalance in your dog's diet. Dog food is formulated as a complete food. Snacks add calories, but if they aren't formulated for dogs, they provide lots of calories and not much nutrition.

> **Dog Treats**
> ### Cheese Bone Cookies
> 2 cups all-purpose flour
> 1 1/4 cup cheese, any kind, shredded
> 2 garlic cloves, minced
> 1/2 cup vegetable oil
> 4 TB. water
>
> Preheat oven to 400°F. Combine flour, cheese, garlic, and oil, knead well. Add water, if needed, to form stiff dough. Roll out on floured surface to 1/2" thick, cut into shapes. Place on ungreased cookie sheet. Bake 10 to 15 minutes or until bottoms are lightly browned. Cool on wire rack. Refrigerate in airtight container.
>
> Courtesy of *Canine Classified*, Anne Page, reprinted with permission.

Wean Rover off the junk food now. If you have to share your spaghetti, pizza, steak, and hamburger, keep the portions very small and no more than half of his treat allowance.

But what about table scraps? My parents routinely tell me that they fed table scraps to their dogs when growing up. But how long did those dogs live? Table scraps are generally the inedible portions of the dinner or stuff that you didn't finish. Table scraps are high in fat, carbohydrates, sugar, and salt—not what a growing puppy or adult dog needs. Again, treat table scraps are like junk food: Keep the portions small, less than 5 percent of your dog's diet.

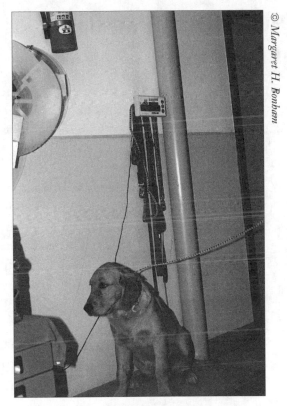

© Margaret H. Bonham

Weight provides a good starting point for whether your dog is fat or fit, but it's better to feel along the ribs and pelvis to determine an actual fitness level.

Should I Use Supplements?

If you feed your dog a balanced diet, there is no need for supplements. In fact, you can cause a serious imbalance in your dog's

> **No Biscuit!**
> Don't add supplements to your dog's diet unless there is a real deficiency. You can cause a severe imbalance or deficiency by supplementing.

diet with "more is better" thinking. As a rule, don't supplement your dog's diet unless your dog is deficient in something— and only do so under the guidance of a vet.

The Ol' Switcheroo—How Do I Change Dog Foods?

Generally, you want to keep your dog on the same dog food; changing foods might cause him to get diarrhea or an upset stomach. However, occasionally, you may wish to switch dog foods. Perhaps it

> **Dog Treats**
> Switch your dog to a new food by mixing the following ratio of new to old dog food each day:
> 10%/90%
> 20%/80%
> 30%/70%
> 40%/60%
> 50%/50%
> 60%/40%
> 70%/30%
> 80%/20%
> 90%/10%
> On the 10th day, feed 100 percent of the new dog food. This will minimize stomach upsets and diarrhea.

is because the breeder fed one type of puppy food and you want your puppy to be on another, or maybe it's time for your puppy to switch to an adult dog food (at about a year old). Or maybe that hoity-toity dog food that you've been feeding from Chez Haute Cuisine is no longer available. Whatever the case, you need to switch over and want to do it without causing diarrhea or an upset stomach.

The best way to change your dog's diet is gradually. Start him out with about 10 percent of the new food and mix it with about

90 percent of the old. Increase the new food by 10 percent while decreasing the old food by about the same percentage every couple of days. This should minimize his chances of having diarrhea and stomach upsets.

How Do I Handle a Picky Pooch?

If your dog is usually a good eater but suddenly becomes picky, this may be a sign of a serious problem. A trip to the vet is in order to see what is causing your pooch to be picky.

Other causes for being picky include tooth problems, gastric upsets, or allergies to certain foods. You should rule out these causes before you decide to switch dog foods to entice your dog to eat.

Picky dogs tend to be made, not born, although I suspect there are some naturally picky dogs out there. If your dog turns up his nose at his dog food, is it because you're willing to ladle on the flavorings and table scraps? Do you dole out junk food as much as you do kibble?

Once you've ruled out a medical problem, the best way to cure a picky eater is to go cold turkey. No, not *feed* him turkey—feed him his regular ration of dry kibble without the trimmings. If he doesn't eat in 10 minutes, pick the food up and don't offer it again until his next meal. Don't give him treats or snacks to tide him over, no matter how sad he looks. Give him his next ration and wait 10 minutes. If he doesn't eat then, pick it up again.

> **Dog Treats**
> Rule out possible health problems when faced with a picky pooch. Other possible causes for being picky include changing dog food frequently, giving lots of table scraps and junk food, and not liking the current brand of dog food.

> **Dog Treats**
> A good place to pick up dog food samples is at the vendor booths at dog shows. Sometimes the vendors will sell dog food there at low prices as well.

Sometimes you'll get a stubborn dog who won't eat for a day or two. If your dog still refuses to eat, have him checked over by the vet again or have another vet check him out. The only dog I've ever known whose pickiness wasn't caused by the owner was one with a health problem.

That being said, there *are* dog foods that some dogs simply don't like. I've found one or two that my dogs would eat if there were nothing else, but they evidently thought I was feeding them the brussels sprouts and lima beans of dog food. They became better eaters when I switched dog foods. If you decide to try this, ask if the manufacturer has samples or purchase the smallest amount possible so that you won't be wasting your money if your dog doesn't like it.

Fit or Fat—What Is a Healthy Weight?

Your dog should not be overweight. Like obesity in humans, obesity in dogs is unhealthy. If your dog is overweight, he is at a much higher risk of developing weight-associated diseases. He is more injury prone and the extra weight can aggravate conditions such as hip and elbow dysplasia.

Most pet dogs are obese. Too often, their owners dole out their love in too much dog food, treats, and snacks. The average sedentary pet seldom needs the amount of food for an active or working dog. Many owners feed high-calorie performance foods and fail to cut back the rations.

Although weighing your dog provides a good baseline when comparing him to the breed standard, this does not provide a good measure for a dog's fitness. Body structure varies from dog to dog, even within a breed, so weight should only be used as a guideline.

The best way to determine your dog's fitness is to put your thumbs on the dog's spine and feel the ribs with your outstretched fingers. You should be able to feel your dog's spine, ribs, and ribcage easily. Moving your hands toward the tail, you should also be able to feel the pelvis. If you cannot feel the spine, ribs, or pelvis or must search to feel them (that is, they are heavily padded), your dog is too fat. Consult your veterinarian. He or she may recommend a special low-calorie diet. If your dog is currently performing in a sport, you may wish to still keep your dog on a premium-performance dog food—just feed him less.

Deciphering Fact or Fiction: Basic Food Fallacies or "Mythconceptions"

So much of our information comes from word-of-mouth that it's tempting to believe things that we hear, no matter how far-fetched. Someone knows someone, who met someone, whose cousin had a dog ... well, you get the picture. Old wives tales and urban legends exist even when it comes to dog food. Take a look at some of the most common fallacies associated with feeding dogs:

- **Your should never feed your dog pork.** I heard this one growing up. In fact, I seem to remember a vet telling my parents that if we fed pork to our dog, she'd get worms. The truth is, pork is an excellent meat—if cooked. In fact, many premium dog foods have pork and lard (pork fat) in their ingredients. Uncooked pork may carry trichinosis, a deadly parasite.

- **Your dog needs a raw egg for his coat.** Raw eggs often contain Salmonella and the raw egg white ties up biotin, an important nutrient. If you want to produce a biotin deficiency in your dog, feed him raw eggs.

- **Dogs should only eat meat.** A dangerous fallacy. While it is true that dogs are carnivores like wolves, wolves don't just eat muscle meat. Wolves eat everything: skin, entrails, contents of the stomach, bones, and organs. Wolves eat predigested plant material from their prey.

- **Dogs do well on a vegetarian diet.** Maybe a housepet will subsist on a vegetarian diet, but remember, wolves don't stalk tofu in the wild. Most dogs digest and metabolize vegetable protein poorly. If your dog needs good nutrition, feed him what his body was designed to process.

- **A dog will get good nutrition from table scraps.** Table scraps are those inedible portions of your meal or your leftovers. Human food is high in salt, sugar, carbohydrates, and fats. In terms of nutritive value, table scraps can't provide a balanced diet.

- **Brewer's yeast and garlic will prevent fleas.** Brewer's yeast is a good source of B vitamins and garlic is a flavor enhancer, but neither will do much to get rid of fleas. It might protect your dog against vampires, though.

- **Raw meat is better for a dog.** This is a partial fallacy. While there is a better nutrition content in raw meat, there is also the potential for E. coli and Salmonella. Raw pork and some raw game meat may contain trichinosis. Raw beaver and rabbit may contain tularemia, a dangerous bacteria, and any raw game may contain tapeworms.

- **Commercial dog food can't supply adequate nutrition.** This is a partial fallacy. Dog food that is formulated to meet or exceed AAFCO guidelines *is* nutritionally complete. If the dog food isn't formulated to AAFCO guidelines, then it isn't complete. Read the label.

 No Biscuit!

Don't believe everything you hear about dogs and dog food. Check with a vet or animal nutritionist before trying something based on hearsay.

- **Dogs will eat what they need so you can leave a bowl out for him to snack on.** This is a common fallacy. Some dogs are able to regulate their food intake, but most will overeat if given the chance. Some dogs, such as sled dogs, will eat until they literally can't hold anymore—this binge eating isn't acceptable. Feed your dog two meals every day—or if a puppy, three meals—so that you can monitor his eating, so he will not get fat and also so that you can tell when he is sick or not.

The Least You Need to Know

- Feed your dog according to the feeding guidelines on the dog food package and adjust according to weight, age, fitness, and activity level.

- Adult dogs need to eat twice daily; puppies younger than six months should be fed three times daily.

- Scheduled mealtimes, rather than free feeding, will help alert you to possible health problems if your dog skips a meal. A dog skipping a meal is a sign that he is having a possible health problem.

- Limit treats to no more than 10 percent of your dog's food. Limit table scraps and junk food to no more than half of your dog's treats.

- If you must switch dog foods, change to the new food gradually to prevent stomach upset and diarrhea.

- Most pets are overweight. Feel your dog's ribs to determine whether he is fit or fat.

Chapter 15

The Nutrients Every Dog Needs

In This Chapter

- 🏠 Learn what nutrients are necessary for a healthy dog
- 🏠 Protein, fat, and carbohydrates and the roles they play in your dog's health and energy
- 🏠 Vitamins and minerals
- 🏠 Water as the most important nutrient

By now, you know that nutrition is very important for your dog, but what nutrition does your dog actually need? What are protein, fat, and carbohydrates and what role do they play in your dog's metabolism?

Just as important as protein, fat, and carbohydrates are vitamins and minerals. It's important to understand their roles in a dog's metabolism as well as the links between certain minerals.

The Vet Is In

The first manufactured dog food was a dog biscuit in 1860 in England.

 Woofs

A **calorie** is a measure of energy. It is the energy required to raise the temperature of a gram of water by 1°C.

A **kilocalorie** is the energy required to raise the temperature of a kilogram of water by 1°C.

In this chapter, I discuss the role vital nutrients play in a dog's health; what happens when a deficiency occurs or when a dog is given too much of a nutrient (some vitamins are toxic); and the important role of water—a vital nutrient.

Proteins and Fats and Carbs, Oh My!

Dogs require energy in the form of *calories*, or rather *kilocalories*. The nutrients that provide energy are proteins, fats, and carbohydrates.

Protein Power

Protein is an essential nutrient. It provides 4 kilocalories per gram and provides the building blocks for muscles, bone, organs, and connective tissue. It is the main component of enzymes, hormones, and antibodies. It helps to repair muscle, to build and maintain plasma volume and red blood cells, and to build mitochondrial volume in working dogs.

Protein is composed of 23 different *amino acids*. Of these 23, a dog's body can manufacture 13. The other 10 amino acids, called *essential amino acids* must come from a dog's nutrition.

The essential amino acids are arginine, histidine, isoleucine, leucine, lysine, methionine, phenylalanine, threonine, tryptophan, and valine. A protein source with all 10 essential amino acids is said to be a *complete protein source*. Protein sources without all 10 are said to be *incomplete protein sources*.

Woofs

Amino acids are the building blocks that make up protein.

Essential amino acids are the amino acids that must be present in a dog's diet to prevent a deficiency.

Nonessential amino acids are the amino acids that are manufactured within a dog's body.

The amino acids must be balanced in such a way that the dog gets enough protein for his body. A combination of plant and animal sources usually offers the most complete diet. Because dogs are carnivores, they digest and use protein from animal products better than from plant sources. Good sources of protein include meat (chicken and poultry included), eggs, meat meal, meat by-products, and meat by-product meals.

According to AAFCO guidelines, puppy food must have 22 percent protein and adult food must have 18 percent protein on a *dry-matter basis* as a minimum requirement.

Woofs

A **complete protein source** is a source of protein that contains all 10 essential amino acids.

The **dry-matter basis** is the percentage or amount of nutrients as compared to the overall weight of the dog food without water.

An **incomplete protein source** is a source of protein that contains only nine or fewer of the essential amino acids.

Fat Burners

Fat is an energy-dense nutrient at 9 kilocalories per gram. High-quality fat sources include animal fat. Dogs use fats that are commonly referred to as Omega-6 long-chained fatty acids. These fats are called Omega-6 because they have a double bond at the sixth carbon atom. They are usually a mixture of saturated (solid) and unsaturated (liquid) fats. Unsaturated fat tends to turn rancid quicker.

Another type of fat is an Omega-3 fat. Its first double chain is at its third carbon atom. Omega-3 fats have many health benefits, including anti-inflammatory qualities and the potential to help decrease the risk of developing certain kinds of tumors and cancers. These fats generally come from fish oils and linseed oils. They tend to turn rancid quickly. However, too much Omega-3 fatty acids can be dangerous. Because of their blood-thinning qualities, Omega-3 fatty acids can inhibit blood clotting in humans if overingested; the potential for hemorrhaging if injured may be too great. Most dogs benefit from diets with no more than 4 to 5 percent of fat on a dry-matter basis coming from Omega-3s.

The Vet Is In

Converting a dog food to a dry-matter basis might be a little confusing, especially if you're working with a canned dog food. Dog food labels are listed on a by-weight basis, meaning that the percentages include the weight of all the ingredients, including water.

The reason you want to compare on a dry-matter basis is that by calculating on a dry-matter basis, you even up the nutrients. This way, you can compare foods regardless of the amount of moisture. This is handy when comparing dry food with canned, for example.

Dry matter, by definition, are the ingredients in the dog food with the water removed. Look at the dog food label under the "Guaranteed Analysis." It will have the word "Moisture" and the percentage. Subtract the moisture from 100% and you have the percentage of dry matter. Now you can determine the percentage of protein and fats.

To determine the percentage of protein on a dry-matter basis, take the percentage of protein and divide it by the percentage of dry matter.

For example, if the protein on a dog food label says 28 percent and the moisture is 10 percent, do the following:

Subtract the moisture from 100 percent. 100−10 = 90 percent dry matter.

Divide the protein percentage by the dry-matter percentage: 28 ÷ 90 = .3111 or about 31 percent protein on a dry-matter basis.

According to AAFCO guidelines, puppy food must have 8 percent fat and adult food must have 5 percent fat on a dry-matter basis as a minimum requirement.

Carb Loading

Carbohydrates are a nutrient that provides 4 kilocalories of energy per gram. Because dogs are primarily carnivores, they need much less carbohydrate than humans. In fact, the AAFCO doesn't have a minimum standard for carbohydrates, which means a dog can live without them.

However, carbohydrates do play an important role, providing energy, fiber, and replacement of a fuel called glycogen within the cells. Fiber helps in water absorption and in maintaining good bowel movements.

Vitamins

My mom always told me to take my vitamins. Vitamins are an important part of a dog's health as well. If a dog food is formulated to AAFCO standards, your dog will have all the vitamins he needs, and there is no reason for you to supplement his diet with extra vitamins.

Here's a rundown of the vitamins required by the AAFCO and the role they play in a dog's health:

- **Vitamin A.** Immune system, eyes, growth and repair of body tissues, skin, hair, and reproduction.

- **Vitamin D.** Bones and teeth.

- **Vitamin E.** Muscle, heart, blood, hormones, and reproduction.

- **Thiamine (B1).** Nervous system.

The Vet Is In
Dogs manufacture vitamin C in their bodies. Whether dogs can actually become deficient in vitamin C is still debatable.

- 🐾 **Riboflavin (B2).** Eyes, skin, nails, nervous system, and hair.

- 🐾 **Pantothenic acid.** Adrenal glands, nervous system, skin, and hair.

- 🐾 **Niacin.** Blood, heart, and nervous system.

- 🐾 **Pyridoxine (B6).** Immune system, nervous system, and blood.

- 🐾 **Folic acid.** Reproduction blood, and bones.

- 🐾 **Vitamin B12.** Blood and nervous system.

- 🐾 **Choline.** Nervous system, blood, and bones.

Besides affecting the above systems, vitamins often play a role in metabolic functions, such as the conversion of glucose into energy, transference of chemicals on a cellular level, and other cellular functions.

The Vet Is In

AAFCO Minimums for Vitamins in Dry Matter mg/kg

Vitamins	Puppy and Adult Food
Vitamin A	1.5 (15 max)
Vitamin D	.00125 (.125 max)
Vitamin E	50 (1,000 max)
Thiamine	1.0
Riboflavin	2.2
Pantothenic acid	10
Niacin	11.4
Pyridoxine (B6)	1.0
Folic acid	.18
Vitamin B12	.022
Choline	1,200

Minerals

Just as important as the vitamins are the minerals in a dog's diet. Some, like calcium, you've probably heard of. Here is a rundown of the basic minerals:

- **Calcium and phosphorus.** Bones and muscle. These two minerals play a crucial role together and require a ratio of approximately 1.5 (1.2 to 2.0) calcium to 1 phosphorus. If either exceeds this ratio, there can be serious problems with the dog's bones, either through thinning or malformation.

- **Potassium.** Nervous system, heart, and cells.

- **Sodium.** Cells and water metabolism.

- **Chloride.** Cells and water metabolism.

- **Magnesium.** Nervous system, muscle, and bones.

- **Iron.** Blood.

- **Copper.** Blood.

- **Manganese.** Bones and reproduction.

- **Zinc.** Skin, hair, bones, muscle, and immune system.

- **Iodine.** Thyroid.

- **Selenium.** Bones and heart.

Minerals are essential to a healthy dog's diet. However, many minerals, such as calcium and phosphorus, are linked. Excesses of one particular mineral can interfere with the absorption of other minerals and may actually cause deficiencies. Too much phosphorus in the diet compared to calcium will cause a calcium deficiency. Too much zinc will inhibit copper and iron, thus causing a deficiency.

The Vet Is In

The following list contains common names for vitamins and minerals:

- Animal sterol (source of vitamin D)
- Ascorbic acid (vitamin C)
- Biotin (a B vitamin)
- Calcium pantothenate (calcium)
- Choline chloride (choline)
- Ferrous sulfate (iron)
- Folic acid (a B vitamin)
- Inositol (vitamin B complex)
- Niacin, Niacinamide (a B vitamin)
- Potassium iodide (potassium and iodine)
- Pyridoxine hydrochloride (vitamin B6)
- Riboflavin (a B vitamin)
- Thiamine, thiamine hydrochloride, thiamine mono-nitrate (a B vitamin)
- Tocopherol, a-tocopherol acetate (vitamin E)
- Vitamin A acetate, vitamin A palmitate
- Zinc oxide, zinc sulfate, zinc gluconate (zinc)

Because of this, it is very important that you feed your dog a balanced diet and not supplement unless there is an obvious deficiency. In this case, more isn't better.

Cool, Clear, Water ...

Water is the most important nutrient for your dog. Your dog cannot live long without it. Every major system throughout the body uses water and your dog needs water from a good source every day.

The Vet Is In

AAFCO Minimums and Maximums for Minerals in Dry Matter

Minerals	Units (min/max)	Puppy (min/max)	Adult
Calcium	g/kg	10/25	6/25
Phosphorus	g/kg	8/16	5/16
	Ca/P ratio	1.5:1	11.5:1
Potassium	g/kg	6	6
Sodium	g/kg	3	.6
Chloride	g/kg	4.5	.9
Magnesium	g/kg	.4/3	.4/3
Iron	mg/kg	80/3000	80/3000
Copper	mg/kg	7.3/250	7.3/250
Manganese	mg/kg	5	5
Zinc	mg/kg	120/1000	120/1000
Iodine	mg/kg	1.5/50	1.5/50
Selenium	mg/kg	.11/2	.11/2

If your dog doesn't get enough water, he becomes dehydrated. Dogs lose water through respiration (breathing), urination, defecation, and through the sweat glands in their paw pads. Dehydration can be a serious problem, not only in summer but in winter as well.

If your dog is an athlete, he cannot perform optimally if he is dehydrated. Even mild dehydration can severely affect performance, so it is very important that your dog gets enough water.

Always have fresh water available at all times, and make sure it comes from a known good source. Streams and creeks may contain giardia (see Chapter 9) or other organisms that may cause severe diarrhea and vomiting.

Dehydration can occur at any time of the year. During the hot summer months, a dog will drink water, but dehydration can also occur in the winter months, especially if the air is cold and dry. If you live in cold climates, you can purchase an electrically heated bowl or a water bucket heater to provide water year-round.

Some dogs may not drink enough water in the wintertime and may have to be coaxed into drinking. This is true for canine athletes such as sled dogs. One way to coax them to drink is through baiting—that is, adding a little something extra to the water. Sled dog racers routinely add dog food, beef broth, or pieces of meat to the water to get dogs to slurp it down.

You can check for dehydration by doing a simple skin snap test. While your dog is healthy (and hydrated), gently pull up the skin on the back of the neck and release. The skin should snap back in place. If it "melts" back in, or worse, stays where it is, the dog is dehydrated. Dogs at different ages and different breeds may show different results, so it is important to do this first while the dog is healthy to get a possible gauge. Another place to try this snap test is to use the upper lip and jowl.

The Least You Need to Know

- Follow AAFCO guidelines for protein and fat dry-matter percentages for your puppy or adult dog.

- Dogs obtain energy from protein, fats, and carbohydrates.

- Animal products are generally good protein sources for dogs.

- Fats can be saturated or unsaturated. The common types are Omega-6 long chain fatty acids and Omega-3 fatty acids.

- There is no minimum for carbohydrates in the AAFCO guidelines; however, dogs use carbohydrates for fiber and energy.

- You should always have fresh water available for your dog.

Chapter 16

Reading a Dog Food Label

In This Chapter

- Learn what a dog food label really says
- Understand how to read a Guaranteed Analysis
- Identify general ingredients and digestibility
- Highlight the preservatives used in dog food

You understand the importance of nutrition in dog food—but how does it relate to the actual bag or can of dog food in your pantry? What is Animal Digest, poultry, or tocopherols? How does the Guaranteed Analysis apply to dog nutrition?

In this chapter, I decipher the dog food label and give you an idea of what ingredients are listed in a bag of dog food. When you look at your dog's food and compare it to other brands, you can have a better idea of what actual nutrition is going into your dog.

Dog Food Label Basics

It's not intentional that dog food labels are so doggone hard to read. The labels are required to be that way by the FDA (Food and Drug

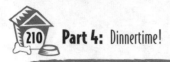

Administration). When you pick up a package of dog food, you'll see a number of various required pieces of information. These include the …

🏠 Product name.

🏠 Manufacturer's name and address.

🏠 Net quantity in weight.

🏠 Guaranteed Analysis.

🏠 Nutritional adequacy statement.

🏠 Feeding directions.

🏠 Ingredients.

No Biscuit!

Premium and Super-Premium mean little on a dog food bag, despite the connotations. Dog food companies can use these terms without regulation, and while they imply better ingredients, they may share some of the same ingredients found in lesser-quality dog food.

There is other information that the dog food manufacturer may put on the label including calories and digestibility, but this is voluntary and at the sole discretion of the company.

What's in a Name?

The product name is the way you recognize the dog food. It's also a way for you to determine the type of dog food you're buying. Depending on your preference, you may be looking for particular types of ingredients, such as beef, chicken, or lamb. Be careful, though! If there is a qualifier on the name, such as "dinner" or "formula," or worse, "with" or "flavor," you may see less of that actual ingredient in the dog food than you would expect.

Here are some examples of how an ingredient can be used in a name:

🏠 If the ingredient is mentioned in the product name with no qualifier (such as "dinner" or "formula"), then that ingredient

must comprise at least 95 percent of the dog food. For example, if the dog food says "Beef Dog Food" as its title, then the dog food must be made from 95 percent beef.

🐾 If the ingredient or ingredients are in the title as "dinner," "formula," "nuggets," or some other qualifier, then the ingredients mentioned must be 25 percent of the dog food. Of that 25 percent, one of the ingredients must be at least 3 percent of the 25 percent total and must be listed in order. So, a "Lamb and Rice Formula for Dogs" is at least 25 percent lamb and rice, with neither less than 3 percent.

🐾 If the food states "with," as in "with beef" or "with lamb," the ingredient only has to be 3 percent of the total food.

🐾 "Flavored" does not have to have a percentage, but must exist in the dog food. "Beef Flavored" could have very little beef in it.

Somewhere on the label should also be the manufacturer's name and address. There may be a distributor name and address as well.

Also on the product should be the weight, for comparison with other dog foods.

Basic Percentages: Guaranteed Analysis

The *Guaranteed Analysis* is a statement that shows the percentages of protein, fat, water, and other ingredients in a dog food "as is."

The Guaranteed Analysis states the following on the label:

🐾 The minimum percentages of crude protein

🐾 The minimum percentages of crude fat

Woofs

The **Guaranteed Analysis** is a statement that shows the percentages of protein, fat, water, and other ingredients in a dog food "as is."

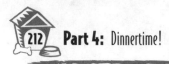
🏠 The maximum percentages of crude fiber

🏠 The maximum moisture or water

These percentages are listed "as is" or "as fed" percentages, sometimes called "by-weight." Some dog foods will list *ash* as well. These percentages guarantee a certain amount of protein and fat. However, they don't guarantee the quality of the ingredients. Protein, through this type of analysis, can be from indigestible or digestible ingredients. For example, an old shoe will show a certain amount of protein, but whether it can be used by your dog is another story.

Woofs

Ash is a general term for the residue (total mineral content) remaining after a dog food has been tested in the laboratory through burning.

When comparing the protein and fat content of various dog foods, look at them on a dry-matter basis. This requires that you convert the percentages to dry matter (see Chapter 15). Once you convert the dog food to dry matter, you can compare any dog food with any other.

Ingredients List

When you look at the ingredient list on dog food, you'll see that the ingredients are listed according to weight. So, the first ingredient is the most prevalent ingredient, followed by the second most prevalent, and so forth. With most dog foods, you'll want the protein source to be listed first, followed by other ingredients.

If the first ingredient is chicken, does this mean that the food is mostly chicken? Not necessarily. For example, suppose a dog food contained, as the first five ingredients, chicken, corn, corn gluten meal, wheat middlings, and poultry fat (preserved with BHA). The corn, corn gluten meal, and wheat middlings, taken together, may outweigh the chicken. Also, when the term "chicken" is used, it includes the water that is in the chicken, whereas chicken meal and chicken by-product meal have water and fat extracted. Technically, chicken meal could have a higher percentage of available protein than chicken on a pound-for-pound basis.

The Vet Is In

The following is a short list of definitions in the AAFCO guidelines, modified for this book.

- **Meat.** The clean flesh of slaughtered mammals. It is limited to muscle meat, without organs, except the heart, tongue, diaphragm, and esophagus.

- **Poultry.** The clean combination of flesh and skin with or without bone, derived from part or whole carcasses, exclusive of feathers, heads, feet, and entrails.

- **By-Products.** The words "by-products" often have negative meanings for pet owners. By AAFCO definition, the term "Meat by-products" is the nonrendered, clean parts other than meat, from slaughtered mammals. It includes all organs and defatted fatty tissues. It does not include stomach or intestine contents, hair, horns, teeth, and hooves. While this sounds rather unappetizing to us humans, by-products provide high-quality protein.

- **Meat Meal.** Is the ground form of the meat. It does not contain blood, hair, hoof, hide, manure, stomach, or rumen contents. The meat has water and fat extracted. If the label says "chicken meal," then the meal must be made from chickens.

- **Animal Digest.** Another misunderstood protein source is *Animal Digest.* By AAFCO definitions, it is a material that results from chemical and/or enzymatic hydrolysis of clean, undecomposed animal tissue. The animal tissue is exclusive of hair, horns, teeth, hooves, and feathers except in such trace amounts as might occur unavoidably in good factory practice and are suitable for animal feed.

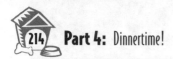

Nutritional Adequacy Statement

For a dog food to be "complete and balanced," it must adhere to the AAFCO guidelines and must include some statement to that effect. There are two ways a dog food may be proven complete. One is to provide proof that the levels of nutrients meet the established AAFCO profile. The other way is through feeding trials.

One of these two statements should appear on the package:

🏠 <Dog food name> is formulated to meet the nutritional levels as established by the AAFCO Dog Food Nutrient Profiles.

🏠 Animal feeding tests using AAFCO procedures substantiate that <dog food name> provides complete and balanced nutrition.

 Dog Treats
Because the quality of the dog food ingredients relies heavily on the manufacturer, look for a manufacturer committed to producing a quality product.

 **No Biscuit!**
AAFCO definitions of ingredients do not define the quality of the ingredient. The ingredients vary according to the source and manufacturer.

 Dog Treats
AAFCO has an entire book dedicated to definitions of ingredients and regulations. You can purchase their regulations on their website at www.aafco.org.

Feeding Directions

The dog food manufacturer should provide some type of guideline in feeding your dog, usually in cups per pound of body weight or cups for a certain weight range and age.

These guidelines are just that—guidelines. Most pet food companies pad the amount because they wish to take into account all possible breeds and metabolisms. You should start with the recommended amount and reduce or increase as required.

Digestibility

Because protein and fat are crude, it is not all necessarily digestible or metabolized. The ingredient's quality determines digestibility. Many premium pet foods claim a certain percentage digestibility, such as 85 or 90 percent digestible. The higher the digestibility, the more the dog is going to use the nutrients.

The problem is, there is no way to tell if a bag of dog food has quality ingredients just by looking at the ingredients list or Guaranteed Analysis. The difference between by-products from one manufacturer may be vastly different than the by-products another manufacturer uses. The way to tell is to find out the digestibility. Most manufacturers have those numbers available and you can contact the manufacturers directly (phone, e-mail, or mail).

Natural Foods

What about so-called "natural foods"? If you are looking for your pet's food to be minimally processed, coming from 100 percent natural sources, organically grown, and without pesticides, steroids, and antibiotics, then you may have to formulate your pet's food. Commercial natural foods are often preserved with tocopherols, have no artificial flavors and colors, and often are made with ingredients that some dogs are sensitive to such as corn, wheat, poultry, and beef.

What's more, many vitamins and minerals you can't get from their natural sources—you have to synthesize them in a laboratory. So, the whole "natural" concept disappears when talking about a complete and balanced commercial diet.

"Natural" is an overused word in labeling. "Natural Flavors," for example, can be concocted in a laboratory and as long as they are the same flavoring that occurs naturally in the wild, they can be considered "natural." (Haven't you ever wondered how something could have no fruit juice and still be "natural strawberry flavored"?)

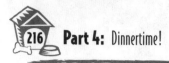

AAFCO has written guidelines for labeling "natural" pet food. The unqualified use of the word "natural" cannot be used if any ingredients are chemically synthesized. Pet food manufacturers may use the word "natural" if qualified that all ingredients are not chemically synthesized, except vitamins and minerals. They must add a disclaimer saying something like "natural with added vitamins and minerals." Pet food labels may also use the term "natural" in a specific ingredient, such as "preserved naturally with vitamin E" or "natural beef flavor."

Preservatives

Arguably, the biggest pet food debate in recent years has been the ethoxyquin controversy. However, many holistic vets and some breeders believe that most chemical preservatives, including ethoxyquin, are bad for your pet. The bad press has caused several dog food manufacturers to switch their preservatives to tocopherols— a form of vitamin E.

The disadvantage to this is the product's shelf life. Vitamin E does not preserve fat as well as some chemicals, and consequently there is a greater chance of rancidity. If the manufacturer, shippers, or distributors store the dog food in a hot building or for too long, the food can become rancid. At the very least, the food may not provide the proper nutrition, and may make your pet sick.

Common chemical preservatives include: BHA, BHT, propyl gallate, ascorbic acid, calcium sorbate, sodium benzoate, sodium nitrite, sodium ascorbate, citric acid, tocopherols, and benzoic acid.

Preservatives are somewhat controversial. Most preservatives have a shelf life of less than one year. Tocopherols (a mixture of vitamin E), ascorbic acid (vitamin C), and citric acid tend to be touted as safer than other preservatives because they're naturally occurring substances in foods.

The Least You Need to Know

🏠 The Food and Drug Administration requires that dog food be labeled a certain way to include the brand name, manufacturer's name and address, weight, Guaranteed Analysis, nutritional adequacy statement, ingredient list, and feeding directions.

🏠 The words "premium" and "super-premium" have no definition on a dog food label according to the FDA.

🏠 The Guaranteed Analysis gives minimum crude protein and crude fat, but does not state whether those nutrients are available to the dog.

🏠 The AAFCO requires certain definitions in ingredients, but does not guarantee the quality of these ingredients.

🏠 You need to look for dog food that is 85 percent or more digestible.

🏠 The AAFCO has written guidelines for labeling "natural" pet food. The unqualified use of the word "natural" cannot be used if any ingredients are chemically synthesized.

🏠 Although ethoxyquin has been much maligned as a preservative, there is no proof that it is harmful.

Part 5

Nutrition Nuggets

Sometimes good nutrition isn't enough. Dogs, like people, suffer from obesity and other nutritionally related problems. Likewise, not all dogs should be fed the same. A sled dog requires a vastly different diet than the canine couch potato.

In Part 5, we cover diets. Not just weight-reduction diets (although we cover those, too), but what to feed when your pet has special needs and what problems may arise out of his diet.

We also cover homemade diets and the latest fad, raw diets. Are they as good as proponents claim and are they based on sound research? What are the pitfalls associated with them?

Finally, we cover feeding your dog. Is he a puppy or an adult? Working dog or senior? Couch potato or canine athlete? Each activity and age level requires special feeding.

Chapter 17

Diet Isn't "Die" with a "T"

In This Chapter

- Why obesity is a growing problem among dogs
- How to talk to your vet about putting your dog on a diet
- How prescription diets can help
- The importance of exercise

Pudgy puppies aren't healthy, and if your dog suffers from obesity, he's likely to live a shorter life. Obesity is a growing problem among pets as dog owners dole out their love in the form of cookies, snacks, table scraps, and other treats.

That extra weight can stress joints—an important factor if your dog has joint problems, such as hip or elbow dysplasia or arthritis. Dogs that are obese are more likely to suffer from diabetes and congestive heart failure.

In this chapter, I cover obesity in dogs—how they get there and what you can do about trimming a pudgy puppy.

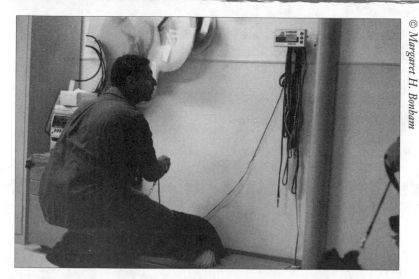

© *Margaret H. Bonham*

Ask your vet if your dog is heavy. He can recommend a special diet and exercise program for your dog.

Obesity—a Growing Problem with Dogs

We're encouraged to feed our dogs. (How many dog food ads do you see in dog magazines and sponsoring animal shows?) We certainly don't want to starve them, so we're naturally encouraged to buy and feed more pet food.

And, of course, our dogs know a good thing when they see it. They practice those soulful, starved looks when you're asleep or at work. I'm sure my dogs sit behind me and plot how to coerce my dinner or snacks from me. I'm sure your dog does, too. It's a canine conspiracy.

 No Biscuit!

The standard weight for your dog's breed should not be used to gauge whether your dog is svelte or swelled. Instead, feel for your dog's ribs and look for a tuck at the abdomen.

Just because your dog weighs within the standard for his breed doesn't mean that he is fit. His correct weight should be in proportion to his build. You should be able to feel his ribs easily and even his hip bones. If your dog appears to be "ribless" to the touch, you can bet he needs to shed a few pounds. A dog should have a good "tuck" at the abdomen—if your dog looks more like a barrel, he may benefit from losing weight.

As a sled dog racer, I'm more sensitive to overweight dogs. Extra weight in dogs can not only slow the dogs down, but can be downright dangerous by overstressing their hearts. Still, I've had dogs that have been more than a few pounds overweight.

No Biscuit!
A fat puppy isn't a healthy puppy. That extra weight can stress the joints and in some cases cause malformations.

The good news is, because it isn't you dieting, you can regulate your dog's weight easily. While it may be hard to say no to the ice cream or extra slice of pizza, you can become exceedingly virtuous with your dog. Go ahead, have that extra slice of pizza—just don't give it to your dog!

Dog Treats
Sometimes just cutting out the junk food—the table scraps and treats—is all that's required to trim down a pudgy pup.

Weighing In—Discussing a Diet with Your Vet

Most vets are used to seeing fat dogs. It's rare to see a vet who is used to canine athletes and their trim builds, although they are out there. As a result, many vets think that an overweight dog is okay.

Most vets are happy to see your dog at all, regardless of how plump he rolls in. At an annual checkup, ask your vet for an honest evaluation of your dog's weight. If your vet says your dog is heavy, you may want to discuss possible options. If your vet thinks he's fine, but you think he's fat, ask your vet for a careful evaluation.

Always seek your vet's help before putting your dog on a weight-loss diet or exercise program.

Diet Aids—Prescription and "Lite" Weight-Loss Diets

If you have a pudgy pooch, you have several options available. If your dog is getting pudgy because of snacks, the easiest thing to do is cut out those table scraps and treats. Some treats can be full of calories, despite their small size.

Still, you might need a little help. Your vet can prescribe a prescription diet that can help your dog shed those extra pounds. Several dog food manufacturers including Purina, Hill's, and Waltham offer diet foods available to your vet.

Another potential weight-loss food is the "lite" version of dog foods. A new regulation implemented by AAFCO requires that all "lite" or "low-calorie" dog food contain no more than 3100 kcal/kg.

These dog foods work fine provided that you feed the same amount you would with normal food. It does no good to feed "lite" foods if you overfeed them.

However, remember that these dog foods tend to be lower in fat and protein—if your dog is a puppy, canine athlete, or sick, then you shouldn't feed these lower-fat foods without first consulting a vet.

No Biscuit!

Don't put a puppy under 1 year, a canine athlete, or a sick dog on a low-calorie diet unless he's under a vet's supervision.

Of course, another way to cut back your dog's calories is simply to feed him the same food, only feed him less. Most owners do tend to overfeed their dogs, so if you can safely cut back a little, do so.

Exercise—Trimming the Pudgy Pooch

A vital part of keeping your dog fit is exercising him every day. If your dog is a couch potato, exercise will not only help get him in shape, but will also make him a better pet. Your dog will enjoy the activity and the ability to have some fun with you as well as the break in the routine.

© Margaret H. Bonham

Exercise need not be boring or tedious. Playing fetch or other games can help trim a pudgy pooch.

Even a little exercise is beneficial. Depending on your breed, it could just be a walk every day or a game of fetch. Some high-activity dogs require sports such as agility, skijoring, or flyball.

Keep these rules in mind when exercising your dog:

- Have a vet check your dog over before beginning any exercise program. If this is your first time, you may want to have an okay from your doctor, too.

- Start slow, go slow—your dog is enthusiastic, but not in condition. He doesn't know when to stop, so be conservative.

- Be extremely careful in warm weather. Dogs have inefficient cooling systems and cool themselves by panting. If your dog's tongue is dragging, you're working too hard.

- Offer water often. Check for signs of overheating and dehydration.

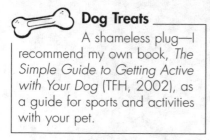

Dog Treats

A shameless plug—I recommend my own book, *The Simple Guide to Getting Active with Your Dog* (TFH, 2002), as a guide for sports and activities with your pet.

- Keep your ego out of it—your dog doesn't care if you jog 1 mile or 5. Take care that he doesn't push too hard.

- Build up slowly. Increase mileage or intensity slowly.

- Do a warmup first to decrease the chance of injury. Just as important is the cooldown.

- Take a break on hot, humid days and don't push your dog. You can usually exercise on hot days in the evenings or early mornings, or if your dog is acclimatized to the weather. Even so, be careful he doesn't overheat or become dehydrated. Also be careful that your dog doesn't burn his pads on hot asphalt or concrete.

The Vet Is In _____

Some sports and activities for dogs include ...

- **Agility.** Completing a dog obstacle course
- **Backpacking.** Hiking with a pack
- **Earthdog.** Finding quarry underground
- **Flyball.** Participating in a relay race that requires your dog to catch a flyball
- **Freestyle.** Dancing with dogs
- **Frisbee.** Catching a flying disc
- **Herding.** Moving stock on command
- **Retrieving.** Retrieving birds or dummies
- **Skijoring.** Having a dog pull a human on skis
- **Tracking.** Searching for "missing" items

The Least You Need to Know

- Most pets are overweight or obese because their owners offer food for love.

- You can easily reduce calories in your dog's diet by cutting the snacks, table scraps, and other treats.

- Obesity can cause many problems including stressing the hips, diabetes, and congestive heart failure.

- Your vet can prescribe a prescription diet, you can feed your dog a "lite" diet, or you may simply need to cut back the amount of food you give him. Always discuss these options with your vet.

- Exercise combined with diet will help trim your pudgy pooch.

- Talk with your vet (and doctor) before starting any diet or exercise program.

- There are many dog sports and activities available for the pet owner.

Food-Related Problems and Special Diets

In This Chapter

- 🏠 Food allergies, diet imbalances, and vitamin deficiencies
- 🏠 Diet-related diseases and conditions
- 🏠 Special prescription diets

You know that diet is very important for your dog, but unfortunately, diet can cause problems as well. If your dog is allergic to ingredients in his food, is fed an improper diet, or has a condition that is affected by diet, it's important to understand how it affects him.

In this chapter, I cover health problems that are associated with diets. I also cover the latest prescription diets available for dogs.

The Vet Is In _____

Allergy or intolerance? Dogs that suffer intolerance to certain foods show it through gas, diarrhea, and digestive upset like people who are lactose-intolerant and can't digest milk sugar.

Allergies generally reveal themselves as skin problems such as hot spots, skin infections, and itchy skin.

Allergies

Food allergies and intolerances are common in dogs. Dogs have shown sensitivity to protein sources such as chicken, beef, eggs, lamb, milk, and soy as well as to carbohydrate sources such as corn and wheat.

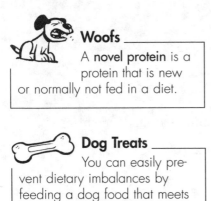

Woofs _____
A **novel protein** is a protein that is new or normally not fed in a diet.

Dog Treats _____
You can easily prevent dietary imbalances by feeding a dog food that meets or exceeds AAFCO standards.

If you think your dog shows a food allergy or intolerance, talk with your vet. He can prescribe a diet with a *novel protein* and carbohydrate source, which you should feed to your dog for a minimum of 12 weeks. If your dog shows improvement, your vet can add a suspect ingredient back into the diet to see if it causes the reaction.

This is really the only conclusive way to test for allergies. Other tests, such as blood tests, aren't accurate enough, though skin tests are more effective.

Bladder Stones

Bladder stones are small crystal stones that build up in a dog's urine within the bladder. There are a variety of causes for bladder stones including diet, age, heavily mineralized water, and other factors.

Your veterinarian may prescribe antibiotics and a urine acidifier. If the bladder stones block the urethra, then surgery is recommended. Bladder stones are often painful and may cause the dog to urinate blood.

Some bladder infections are difficult to cure and may require that the dog be on antibiotics and steroids for several weeks. Low-ash diets and using urine acidifiers will help prevent reoccurrence after surgery.

No Biscuit!

Drinking problem or health problem? If your dog drinks and urinates frequently, it may be a sign of a serious underlying problem, such as …

- **Cushing's disease.** Caused by tumors on the pituitary or adrenal glands. Symptoms include: poor haircoat, excessive drinking and urinating, pot-belly, loss of muscle mass, and a "tragic" look.

- **Diabetes insipidus.** Problem with the ADH (anti-diuretic hormone) levels that causes excessive drinking and urination.

- **Kidney or urinary tract problems.** Caused by damaged kidneys, kidney stones, bladder stones, and infections. May cause excessive drinking/urination, painful urination, or blood in urine.

Bloat

Bloat may or may not be diet-related, although it has been shown that diets high in fiber can aggravate bloating factors. Dogs that eat too much in one sitting and dogs that gulp down food seem predisposed to bloat, as are many large and giant breeds.

Feeding a dog several smaller meals, wetting down the dog food so that it evacuates from the stomach quicker, and not changing food abruptly are all methods of preventing bloat.

Congestive Heart Failure

Although not necessarily linked to diet, many dogs suffer from congestive heart failure due to obesity and the added strain the weight puts on the cardiovascular system. The heart is weakened because of high blood pressure and rapid beating as the heart attempts to pump enough blood to the organs.

Do not put your dog on a diet if he suffers from congestive heart failure without first consulting a veterinarian. A strict diet may actually cause more stress to an already weakened animal. If your dog is obese, talk with your veterinarian about ways to reduce your dog's weight.

Diabetes

Diabetes mellitus is a disease in which the pancreas fails to produce enough insulin to digest carbohydrates and sugars. It is not necessarily linked to diet, but obesity certainly contributes to it. Obese dogs or dogs with poor diets, that is, diets high in sugars and fats, have a greater risk of developing diabetes.

Outward signs include excessive thirst and urination and slow healing. Your vet can make a positive diagnosis through a blood or urine test.

The Vet Is In

Novel protein sources include fish, venison, ostrich, and kangaroo. Novel carbohydrate sources include potatoes, barley, rye flour, and other grains.

If your dog has diabetes, you must make a commitment to caring for him. Type I diabetes requires insulin injections, whereas Type II diabetes does not require insulin, but a change in diet. Regardless of the type of diabetes, your dog will need a restrictive diet. Talk to your veterinarian about methods of caring for a diabetic dog.

Another form of diabetes is known as diabetes insipidus. This is a rare disease that causes a dog to drink and urinate enormous amounts of water. It is a disease of the pituitary gland wherein the body fails to produce enough ADH (antidiuretic hormone). Your vet can diagnose it and it can be treated with medication.

Diet can also help make diabetes more manageable. Talk to your vet about a special diet if your dog has diabetes.

Mineral Imbalances

Mineral imbalances are rare when feeding a complete and balanced diet without supplements. However, if you add meat to your dog's diet or mix in different vitamins, there is a possibility of causing a nutritional imbalance or even a deficiency. Calcium and phosphorus are the primary culprits, but there are other imbalances worth noting.

If calcium and phosphorus become imbalanced, severe calcium deficiencies can result. Over-supplementation can cause bone abnormalities. Other factors can affect calcium absorption, such as too much magnesium and manganese or not enough vitamin D. Too much iron can lead to toxicity and interfere with phosphorous absorption.

If calcium and phosphorus are imbalanced, it can have some pretty devastating effects. Your dog's body will leach the calcium from the bones, thus making them brittle. Photos of animals fed nothing but an all-meat diet are pretty gruesome to look at. Their bones are brittle and deformed, with little actual bone left. Animals with this severe deformity have to be euthanized.

No Biscuit!
Supplementing with meat can cause a serious calcium deficiency if the meat is not balanced with bonemeal.

Other minerals can interfere with each other as well. Too much copper can cause anemia, but too much zinc will cause both a copper and iron deficiency.

Kidney Problems

Most kidney problems are caused by hereditary and congenital conditions (such as Renal Dysplasia, PLE/PLN), kidney stones, and bacterial and viral infections. Excessive protein does not cause kidney damage, but once there is kidney damage you should probably limit your dog's protein intake.

Protein-Losing Enteropathy (PLE) and Protein-Losing Nephropathy (PLN) are two genetic conditions that affect the kidneys. Dogs with these conditions may have skin problems that may otherwise be diagnosed as allergies. Common symptoms of PLE and PLN are vomiting, diarrhea, decreased appetite, weight loss, fluid retention, and lethargy. Dogs with PLE/PLN may drink water and urinate excessively. Blood clots form in some dogs.

Veterinarians should test any dog that exhibits signs of PLE/PLN. Dogs that have this disease should be placed on a gluten-free (no wheat) diet with a novel protein source such as fish, venison, or other protein source not common in dog foods. See Chapter 11 for more information about PLE/PLN.

Pancreatitis

Pancreatitis is a condition in which the pancreas fails to produce enough digestive enzymes. This condition may be chronic or acute. Dogs with pancreatitis may vomit undigested food, show abdominal pain, have grayish, foamy diarrhea or stools, and refuse food.

 No Biscuit!

Excessive fatty foods may bring on an acute attack of pancreatitis. Limit fatty table scraps to avoid pancreatitis.

Feeding fatty foods may bring a sudden onset of pancreatitis. Dogs that raid garbage or are fed table scraps may be more susceptible. Your vet can help treat pancreatitis through diet and medication.

Paneosteitis

Although the precise cause of Pano is unknown, some breeders and vets believe that it is caused by too much nutrition being fed to large and giant breeds. The theory is that the puppy is outgrowing his bones before they have a chance to catch up. To mitigate this effect, some dog food companies have developed a "large" or "giant" breed formula which offers less protein and fat than conventional dog foods.

Vitamin Deficiencies

Like mineral deficiencies and imbalances, vitamin deficiencies can cause serious problems. If your dog is fed a complete and balanced diet, vitamin deficiencies are rare.

Vitamin deficiencies reveal themselves in various ways depending on the vitamin lacking. Here is a list of vitamins and the problems a deficiency can cause your dog:

- **Vitamin A.** Eyesight problems, muscle problems, poor skin and coat. Vitamin A in excess can be toxic.
- **Thiamin (B1).** Seizures, weight loss, and weakness.
- **Riboflavin (B2).** Skin and hair problems, weight loss, and neurological problems.
- **Niacin.** Skin and hair problems, weight loss, and diarrhea.
- **Pantothenic acid.** Weight loss, skin and hair problems, and diarrhea.
- **Pyridoxine.** Weight loss, seizures, and weakness.
- **Vitamin B12.** Anemia.
- **Vitamin D.** Bone deformities, rickets, and poorly developed muscles.

🏠 **Vitamin E.** Muscle degeneration, reproduction problems, heart problems, and bleeding disorders. Excessive Vitamin E is toxic, reducing clotting and absorption of fat soluble vitamins.

The Vet Is In _____

Does protein cause kidney disease? The answer is an unequivocal no! The amount of protein a dog consumes has no bearing on whether the dog gets kidney disease. Sled dogs, for example, are fed high amounts of protein with no signs of increased incidence. You can continue to feed a higher protein diet, provided your dog's activities warrant it.

However, if your dog has kidney disease, it might be wise to reduce the amount of protein he eats if he is inactive to avoid over-stressing the kidneys. Excessive protein is excreted through the kidneys. However, some studies suggest that dogs with kidney disease may need more protein than originally thought. Talk with your vet about what diet might be appropriate for your dog.

Special Diets

Special diets are formulated for dogs with chronic problems or diseases. They're available only through your veterinarian with a prescription. Most of these diets are intended to help mitigate the effects of the disease—most won't cure the dog.

If your dog has a chronic condition, you might wish to talk with your veterinarian about a special diet. Dog food companies have formulated dog foods to help dogs with ailments.

Your vet will be able to tell you if a diet is available for your dog and whether this is a diet you should consider putting your dog on. I've listed some of the available major diets, but no doubt, the dog food companies will invent other diets as time goes on.

Allergy Diets

Allergy diets are specially formulated for dogs with food allergies. This includes allergies that affect the skin and coat. These diets typically contain protein from a novel protein source and grains that generally do not cause allergies. Some pet food manufacturers are devising several hypoallergenic diets so that if a dog is allergic to certain ingredients, the owner can try others.

Cancer Diets

Cancer diets are for dogs suffering from cancer and undergoing chemotherapy. High in protein and fat, these diets help a dog maintain weight.

> **The Vet Is In**
>
> Dog foods tout a variety of benefits. Some include ...
>
> 🐾 **Dental health.** Claims made about reducing plaque and tartar should be reviewed with the Veterinary Oral Health Center and have their logo on the dog food package.
>
> 🐾 **Skin and coat health.** Claims beyond a healthy skin and coat are drug claims and invalid. Example: Claims such as a particular food will cure allergies or prevent flea infestations are drug claims.
>
> 🐾 **Omega-3 fatty acids.** While research has shown that Omega-3s are indeed beneficial, it is not recognized as an essential nutrient.
>
> 🐾 **Glucosamine or other nutriceuticals.** While some nutriceuticals, such as glucosamine, have been shown to be beneficial, others may not be. Talk with your vet before feeding an unusual diet.

Diabetes Diets

Managing Type I and Type II diabetes requires a change in diet. Dogs that are overweight are more prone to diabetes than dogs that are fit. The current trend is to offer fiber to slow the rate of absorption of sugar into the bloodstream from the intestines. These diets are high in fiber and complex carbohydrates and low in sugars. The extra fiber helps the dog lose weight as well.

Heart Diets

These diets are for dogs with chronic heart problems or heart failure. They are typically lower in sodium than other diets.

Intestinal and Pancreatic Diets

These diets are for dogs with gastrointestinal disorders. They are usually bland, with highly digestible protein and carbohydrates and less fat.

Kidney Diets

These diets have been developed for dogs that have kidney disease. They have lower protein and higher fat as well as lower phosphorus and sodium.

Liver Diets

These diets are for dogs with liver disease. Usually lower in protein and sodium, its intent is to reduce stress on the liver.

Recovery Diets

These diets are for dogs that have trouble maintaining weight after sickness or surgery. These diets are typically high in protein, fat, and calories, and are intended to be extremely palatable. These diets are good for dogs that have problems eating because of an underlying health problem.

Urinary Diets

These diets are for dogs that suffer from urinary tract disease and bladder or kidney stones. It has reduced amounts of phosphorus, magnesium, and other minerals that are associated with bladder and kidney stones. It also has a urine acidifier that helps prevent stones from occurring.

Weight-Management Diets

These diets are for obese dogs. These diets are low in fat and calories and high in fiber to help a dog safely lose weight.

The Least You Need to Know

- Food allergies and intolerances can make your dog miserable.

- Your vet can diagnose a food allergy by putting your dog on a hypoallergenic diet for 12 weeks and then slowly add suspected ingredients.

- Your dog's diet can affect diseases such as congestive heart failure, diabetes, and pancreatitis.

- Protein does not cause kidney problems. However, if your dog has kidney disease, your vet may recommend a low-protein/high-fat diet.

- Your vet can prescribe special diets if your dog has illnesses related to the liver, heart, kidneys, and intestine.

Chapter 19

Home Cookin'

In This Chapter

- 🏠 Identifying homemade diets
- 🏠 Understanding the pros and cons of homemade diets
- 🏠 Developing a homemade diet
- 🏠 Balancing a homemade diet
- 🏠 Considerations you should take when using a recommended homemade diet

Homemade and raw diets are becoming extremely popular with a small but vocal faction of dog owners. I cover both in this chapter because both have similar pitfalls to avoid.

One popular diet is the BARF diet—that is, the "Bones And Raw Food" diet.

It's almost a religion with those who espouse the benefits of feeding raw bones and meat to their dogs. Proponents claim that it cures everything from allergies to cancer. They back their statements up with a preponderance of anecdotal data.

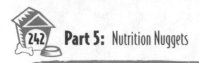
On the other side of the argument is the commercial dog food camp, saying that your dog should eat only commercial dog food—that there are problems associated with homemade diets and you should never feed a homemade diet.

In this chapter, I cover home diets, including the popular BARF (Bones and Raw Food) diet. I'll talk about what works and what doesn't, and what you should do if you're planning to feed your own homemade diet.

Bones are good chews—within reason. Never give your dog a bone that he can swallow whole or that has sharp edges. Marrow bones are usually safe, but even they can chip or fragment.

Pros and Cons to Homemade and Raw Diets

Raw and homemade diets are becoming quite a fad, especially on the Internet. Those who believe in feeding these diets argue that they are better and healthier than anything you could pour from a bag.

Before we get into some myths regarding these diets, let's look at some pros and cons. First, the pros:

🐾 Homemade diets use better ingredients. They're fresher and usually contain human quality ingredients.

🐾 You know what the ingredients are. If you use chicken, you're relatively certain it is chicken. Meat by-products could come from cattle one time and pig the next. There is less chance of feeding your dog something he is allergic to.

No Biscuit!

Before trying out a homemade or raw diet, be certain that it is complete and balanced nutritionally according to AAFCO standards.

🐾 Palatability is usually high. Most dogs love getting fresh meat and vegetables.

🐾 Vitamins are more readily available in raw foods. Vitamins must often be added back after the extrusion process because some of the nutrition is cooked out.

And now, the cons:

🐾 It's expensive. Purchasing and storing the food can cost money and freezer space.

🐾 Bacteria, parasites, and other nasties such as E. coli, Salmonella, and trichinosis abound in raw meat.

🐾 It's time-consuming. It takes time to put together these diets.

🐾 May not be complete and balanced. More on this later.

🐾 Bones may present a health hazard if the dog chews them into pieces and swallows the splinters.

Proponents dismiss each of these con statements as being incorrect or irrelevant. The cost, the price of storage, and the time it takes to fix the food is usually considered irrelevant by proponents. Proponents believe that the bones are passed without harm to the dog and believe that dogs are naturally more resistant to bacteria such as salmonella.

> ### No Biscuit!
>
> Feeding certain raw foods may be downright dangerous to your dog's health.
>
> - Raw egg whites tie up biotin in a dog, causing a serious nutritional deficiency in biotin.
> - Raw pork may carry trichinosis (a deadly parasite).
> - Raw beaver and rabbit may carry tularemia (a serious bacterial infection).
> - Raw game may carry tapeworms.
> - Raw salmon and trout from the Northwest carry a dangerous parasite, *Nanophyetus salmincola*, that causes Salmon Poisoning Disease.

Myths Surrounding Homemade and Raw Diets

Homemade and raw diets have a certain mythology surrounding them. Most consists of testimonials of converts to this new-found diet. Let's take a look at some typical statements:

- **My dog really looks healthier on it.** This is obviously a subjective statement. Healthier than what? Was he sick before the diet? And if he was, what were the other circumstances surrounding his illness? There are too many factors to suggest that this diet alone makes him healthy. Also, the dog looking healthy doesn't tell the whole tale. Is he getting appropriate vitamins and minerals? Is his diet balanced? You can't always tell from looking.

- **My dog had allergies that went away when I started feeding a raw or homemade diet.** The dog was allergic to something in his former diet. Switching to a hypoallergenic diet would do the same thing, as long as the ingredient wasn't present. Raw and homemade diets won't fix a dog whose allergies include ingredients within the raw diet. If your dog is allergic to chicken or beef in a dog food, the problem won't go away if you feed that to him in a raw diet.

🏠 **My dog will be healthier and won't have to go to the vet quite as much.** This is simply not true. A complete and balanced diet will keep your pet healthy, but it will not prevent diseases that a good premium food wouldn't.

🏠 **The raw diet is exactly what a wolf would eat.** No! Wolves don't find carrots or broccoli in the wild. Wolves eat the whole animal, starting with the organs and viscera. They eat the skin and hair, too. Muscle meat—usually the portions people feed along with the bones—isn't everything. Unless you're willing to kill a cow and feed the whole thing—including the ruminant contents—it doesn't simulate anything a wolf would eat. With birds, wolves don't bother plucking the feathers, either, and find the entire bird an appetizing snack.

The other misconception with this is that wolves don't eat little snacks throughout the day, either. They make a kill and gorge up to 20 pounds of meat on a carcass. They may go as long as two weeks without a substantial meal. Wolves aren't long-lived in the wild, either. Wolf pups have up to a 50-percent mortality rate, and it's rare to see a wolf over eight years old.

🏠 **Dogs live longer on a raw diet.** Where are the statistics on this? Dogs live longer with a complete and balanced diet and exercise. I've had several dogs that lived to 15 years old on a commercial diet.

🏠 **Raw bones don't hurt.** Proponents claim that raw bones won't damage a dog's intestines. They feed raw chicken bones, raw beef bones, and whatever else raw to their dogs. Ask any vet and he or she will tell you horror stories about removing a bone that a dog has swallowed. Again, just because wolves eat raw bones doesn't mean it's particularly healthy. Incidentally, the skin and fur eaten with the bones often protects wolves. Without that benefit, a dog could have severe intestinal irritation or damage. Both raw and cooked bones can be dangerous if they are splintered or swallowed whole.

The Vet Is In

Proponents of raw diets tend to compare their diets with wolves. However, most wolves lead pretty rough lives compared to our housepets:

- 🏠 Wolf pups suffer a 50-percent mortality rate.
- 🏠 A wolf can go up to two weeks without a decent feeding.
- 🏠 Wolves can gorge 20 pounds of meat at one meal.
- 🏠 Wolves have an exceedingly high mortality rate in the wild.

🏠 **Dogs have a better resistance to bacteria.** If a dog is used to a certain amount of bacteria present in his diet, then he will naturally have some resistance. Even so, diarrhea may be a common side effect of feeding a raw diet. And just because the dog is resistant doesn't mean you are. You can get E. coli and Salmonella from your dog.

No Biscuit!

Both raw and cooked bones can pose a significant hazard to your dog's health. If you give a bone, make certain it is a large marrow or knuckle bone that your dog can't chew up or swallow.

🏠 **I know how to feed my kids—why not my dog?** Do you feed your kids cereal (fortified with vitamins) in the morning? Do you give your kids vitamins? Do you feed prepackaged foods that are nutritionally enhanced? If you do, then someone has already done the job for you. Even so, some kids are starting to show up with nutritional deficiency diseases like rickets because they're no longer drinking fortified milk and instead

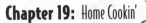

drinking soy and they're using sunblock that filters out vitamin D.

🏠 **The ingredients I buy are better than the chicken feathers [or whatever] used in my dog's food.** If one reads the AAFCO definitions, chicken, chicken by-products, chicken meal, and chicken by-product meal by definition *can't* have feathers in the food. Don't always believe hearsay about what is *really* in dog food. Look at the AAFCO definitions. The dog food would have to say there were feathers [or whatever] in the food.

> **Dog Treats**
> You can make eggs safer by boiling them. Not only will it eliminate the problem of tying up biotin entirely, it also will kill any Salmonella.

> **Dog Treats**
> If you feed a home-made diet, you can greatly improve the balance of vitamins with a good vitamin supplement. Many sled dog racers use wheat germ oil, ground bone meal, and a hematinic such as Canine Red Cell™ in addition to meat, fat, and dog food.

When You Should Consider a Homemade Diet

You should consider a homemade diet if you're faced with the following situations:

🏠 Your dog is allergic or suffers intolerance to ingredients in a commercial diet and there is no comparable hypoallergenic diet available.

🏠 Your dog needs a special diet because of a serious medical condition.

🏠 Complete and balanced dog food is not available or is not formulated to AAFCO guidelines.

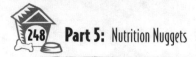
🏠 Your dog is a sled dog and requires in excess of 5,000 kilocalories a day.

Dog Treats

> Pound for pound, commercial dog food is still remarkably inexpensive when comparing it to the ingredients required to concoct a balanced diet. Even at $40 for a 40-pound bag, dog food is less expensive than hamburger and is complete and balanced.

How to Develop Your Own Homemade Diet

If you decide to develop your own homemade diet, start by reading up on nutrition and ingredients. Another step in the right direction is talking to a vet at a veterinary college about nutrition. He or she may be able to provide material to help you design a diet with adequate nutrition for your dog. Some points to keep in mind when developing a diet:

🏠 What is the age of your dog?

🏠 Will the food be cooked or raw? Cooking kills dangerous bacteria but will destroy certain nutrients.

Dog Treats

An alternative to feeding a strictly raw diet is to base your concoction on 10- to 20-percent commercial feed to ensure that your dog is getting some of the right nutrients. You will still have to balance the food once you mix it up. You can get it analyzed at a vet college where they analyze large animal feeds.

🏠 What is the activity level of your dog? If your dog works hard, that is, is a working dog who hunts or pulls a sled, he's going to require far more fat and protein than a sedentary animal.

🏠 Is your dog allergic to or intolerant of certain foods?

🏠 What ingredients are readily available?

🐾 Is your dog's breed predisposed to certain deficiencies, such as zinc?

🐾 Do you have the ingredients necessary to formulate the foods to meet or exceed AAFCO guidelines?

Getting Started

Starting from scratch can be a bit tricky when formulating your own dog food. A first step might be to purchase the AAFCO Official Publication available on AAFCO's website at www.aafco.org.

Consider the nutritional value of certain ingredients. A good human diet book which details the nutritional value of raw ingredients, proteins such as chicken and beef, grains such as oatmeal and wheat flour, and fats such as lard and canola oil, is a must-have.

Be aware that ingredients vary in nutritional value, even between ingredients that claim to have a certain nutrient value. Nutrition varies according to location of where the item was produced, growing or raising conditions, and (in animal products) may even vary from animal to animal.

Dog Treats
You can purchase the AAFCO Official Publication for a little over $50 on AAFCO's website at www. aafco.org.

Talking with a Veterinary Nutritionist

As you start to develop a diet, the next step should be to have a veterinary nutritionist look over your diet for possible suggestions. Even if the nutritionist charges a fee, it's worth him taking a quick look-see to be certain you've got the right amounts of minerals, vitamins, and of course, protein, fats, and carbs.

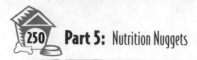

Balancing Act—the Right Nutrients

Look at the amounts of nutrients required in a dog's food listed in Chapter 15. These are minimums required, although a few vitamins, like A and D, have maximums. Pay particular attention to the ratios required in certain minerals like calcium and phosphorus. For example, if the phosphorus level is too high, you could cause a serious calcium deficiency.

Having Your Food Analyzed

Many dog food companies run analyses on each batch of dog food produced to make certain that the formulation meets certain quality requirements. When you develop a diet, you should take the food to a veterinary college for analysis. Most large animal vet colleges can run a protein/fat/carbohydrate analysis and a mineral analysis for a reasonable charge. (Most do feed analyses for stock and horses.) A vitamin profile is very expensive, but may be worth it if you've settled on a diet.

> **No Biscuit!**
>
> Don't believe that throwing your dog an uncooked chicken leg with some carrots and celery is going to provide the correct nutritional balance. Do research, figure out the right portions of meat and other ingredients, and then have them tested to ensure the correct diet.

The Least You Need to Know

- It is very difficult to balance a homemade diet.
- Raw diets are unproven as viable diets with only anecdotal evidence to support their usefulness.
- Many claims made by those who feed raw diets are unsubstantiated.

- Small bones—raw or cooked—can pose a serious danger to your dog if he swallows them. Make sure you give him only a large marrow or knuckle bone that he can't chew up or swallow.

- Raw diets can harbor parasites and bacteria that can be harmful to both you and your dog.

- When designing your own diet, consider purchasing the AAFCO regulations and feeding a diet that meets or exceeds these guidelines.

- Talk with a vet nutritionist and perhaps even have the diet analyzed to be certain it has the right amount of protein/fat/carbohydrates and the right mineral balance.

- Cooking food does make it safer, but it destroys some of the vitamins within the food.

- A potential compromise is to feed a high-quality dog food and add raw components.

Chapter  20

Selecting the Right Food and Diet for Your Dog

In This Chapter

- Types of puppy food
- Types of adult dog food
- Food for performance dogs
- Sled dog diets

Dog food has changed considerably, even within the past 30 years. Back when I was a child, you had puppy food and dog food, and that's about it. There were no real "premium" markets, no specialized foods, and very few choices.

Today, you can purchase dog food that is not only appropriate for a dog's age, but for his activity level, breed, and special needs.

In this chapter, I discuss choosing the right diet for your dog based on his age and needs.

Puppies need a highly digestible premium puppy food. Most puppy foods are 28 protein/18 fat by weight.

Selecting the Right Food

If you're a first-time dog owner, the challenge of choosing a dog food from among the plethora of choices has no doubt left you in shock. Yes, there was a time when dog food was as simple as opening up a bag and pouring it in a bowl. Today you not only have choices of dry, canned, frozen, dehydrated, semisoft, or meat rolls, but you have to figure out what type of diet is best for your dog. Gone are the days of choosing between puppy food and adult food. Now even each age group has its divisions.

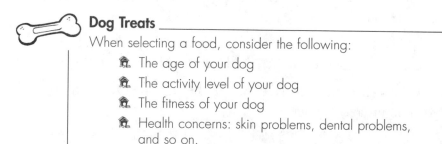

Dog Treats _____

When selecting a food, consider the following:

- 🏠 The age of your dog
- 🏠 The activity level of your dog
- 🏠 The fitness of your dog
- 🏠 Health concerns: skin problems, dental problems, and so on.

Selecting the Right Food for Your Puppy

Growing pups need more nutrition than adults. Although the AAFCO guidelines require that puppy food have a minimum of 22 percent protein and 8 percent fat on a dry-matter basis, most puppy food contains larger amounts of both.

It used to be that one puppy food fit all. Usually a standard premium dry puppy food would have close to 28 percent protein and 18 percent fat as-fed. Now puppy food is specialized to meet the needs of certain breeds.

The Vet Is In

Should you go with a formula suited to a large breed if you have a Newfoundland? Should you go with the small breed if you have a Lhasa Apso? Or should you go with a standard food? It's up to you. Regardless of your breed, the food is still formulated to AAFCO guidelines as a growth formula.

Large Breed

The latest innovation in puppy food is the large breed puppy food. Puppies that are either of large or giant breeds tend to grow quickly and excessive weight can seriously stress their still-developing joints. These dog foods are designed to reduce the amount of nutrition to slow growth and to keep excess weight off. Some large breed formulas contain glucosamine, a nutriceutical that aids in joint health. Protein tends to be 26 to 28 percent as-fed and fat tends to be 13 to 15 percent as-fed.

Medium Breed or Standard Puppy Food

Medium breed or standard puppy food is usually what used to be the standard puppy food offered by dog food companies. Protein tends to be 27 to 30 percent as-fed and fat tends to be 17 to 20 percent as-fed.

Small Breed

Another innovation in puppy food is the small or toy breed puppy food. These are formulated higher in protein and fat because toys grow to their full size in as little as 6 to 8 months. Protein tends to be 30 to 34 percent as-fed and fat tends to be 18 to 20 percent as-fed.

How to Feed Your Puppy

Most puppies younger than 6 months should have their meals split up into three or more feedings. Their stomachs can't handle large portions of dog food at once. Feed according to feeding guidelines on the package and adjust accordingly.

When you feed your puppy, you should pick the same time and same place every day for his meals. Many puppy owners use the puppy's crate as a place to feed him because it rewards him for staying inside the crate. If you have other dogs, feeding your puppy in his crate might be a good idea. It keeps the other dogs away from his food and gives him a welcome chance to eat in private.

No Biscuit!

Don't supplement your puppy's diet with calcium and vitamin C, unless told otherwise by a vet. Excesses can be just as dangerous as deficiencies.

No Biscuit!

Excessive amounts of vitamin C have caused osteoporosis in puppies.

Supplements

Many breeders and puppy owners believe in supplements. Calcium and Vitamin C are two favorites. Supplementing your puppy's diet with calcium can cause growth problems and can inhibit other vitamins and minerals from being absorbed. Vitamin C is manufactured by a dog's body and doesn't need to be supplemented. Too much vitamin C may cause osteoporosis.

© Margaret H. Bonham

Active adults need enough protein and fat for their activities. Most active adult food is 26 protein/15 fat by weight.

Selecting the Right Food for Your Adult Dog (Over 1 Year)

Just as there isn't plain old puppy food anymore, there isn't plain old adult dog food. You have different breed formulas, formulas for losing weight (lite food), senior formulas, performance formulas, skin-and-coat formulas, dental formulas, active adult formulas, and maintenance formulas.

The standard food for adult dogs is active adult. This food is appropriate for active dogs that get moderate amounts of exercise. Maintenance food is for the couch potato that gets little more activity than a walk or a jog to the kibble bowl. Lite food is for dogs that must lose weight. Senior is for older dogs that don't get much exercise.

The Vet Is In

If your dog is.....	Feed him
Under one year	Puppy (breed specific if necessary)
Active	Active Adult (breed specific if necessary)
Gets some exercise	Maintenance
Working or active in sports	Performance
Over 8 years and slowing down	Senior
Overweight	Lite
Has tartar buildup	Dental Diet
Dry skin or coat	Skin and coat

Large Breed

Like large breed puppy food, large breed adult food contains lower protein and lower fat. These dog foods are designed to reduce the amount of nutrition to keep excess weight off to prevent joint problems. Some large breed formulas have glucosamine, a nutriceutical that aids in joint health. Protein tends to be 23 to 26 percent as-fed and fat tends to be 12 to 15 percent as-fed.

Medium Breed (or Regular Active Adult)

Medium breed or regular active adult food is usually what's used to be the standard active adult food offered by dog food companies. Protein tends to be 25 to 26 percent as-fed and fat tends to be 14 to 16 percent as-fed.

Small Breed

Like toy breed puppy food, small breed active adult food tends to be higher in protein and fat. Protein tends to be 26 to 29 percent as-fed and fat tends to be 15 to 18 percent as-fed.

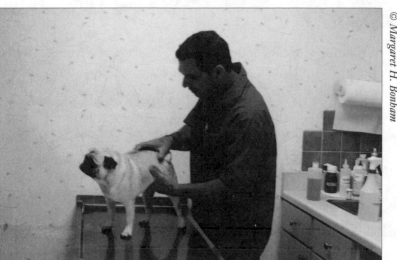

Less-active dogs, such as pets, may do well with a maintenance-type dog food.

Maintenance

Maintenance foods are for less active dogs that maybe get a walk every day and a quick trip to the dog food bowl. They're couch potatoes, preferring to spend time with you on the couch rather than exercise. These foods tend to be 20 to 23 percent protein as-fed and 10 to 12 percent fat as-fed.

Lite

Lite foods are for dogs that need to lose weight. They cannot be more than 3,100 Kcals/kg. These foods tend to be 18 to 22 percent protein as-fed and 8 to 10 percent fat as-fed.

Dog Treats

Don't necessarily switch your dog to a senior diet when he is 8 or older. If your dog is active and maintaining a good weight, keep him on the food you're currently feeding him.

Senior Diets

Senior diets are for sedentary dogs over the age of 8 years. These diets are lower in fat and calories than active adult, and may or may not be lower in protein.

Just because your dog is older doesn't necessarily mean he should be on a senior diet. I've fed sled dogs that were active and healthy on performance foods well past 10 years old.

Specialty Diets

Specialty diets include skin-and-coat diets and dental diets. The AAFCO and FDA do not have an evaluation for skin-and-coat diets, so claims that these foods improve either are largely unsubstantiated. Hypoallergenic diets are only hypoallergenic if the dog is not allergic to the ingredients therein. Many skin-and-coat diets have either novel protein and carbohydrate sources, or fatty acids intended for a healthy coat, such as Omega-3s.

Unless your dog has allergies, a good complete and balanced dog food should naturally produce a shiny, healthy coat.

Dental products must be proven to perform in order to have the logo of the Veterinary Oral Health Center on its package.

Adult Feeding Schedules

Feed your adult dog two or three times a day. Some people feed their dog once a day, but this is usually too large of a meal and may contribute to bloating. Feed your adult dog according to the Feeding Guidelines listed on the dog food container and adjust accordingly.

How to Feed Your Adult Dog

Choosing the same time and same place to feed your dog is a good idea whether he is a puppy or an adult. If you have multiple dogs, sometimes placing their food in "their spot" will cut down on growls and food filching. However, some dogs may need to be fed in their crates where they can't intimidate others.

I've had as many as eight dogs in the house. Dinnertime can be a bit of a chore, especially if you have several. Each dog has his or her own place for food. If one dog is a bully, crate that dog with his dinner so he can't steal someone else's.

> **Dog Treats**
> Don't expect miracles when you switch dog foods. Studies have shown that a dog must be fed the same diet for 6 weeks or more for it to show in his health and energy level.

Feeding Your Canine Athlete

Is your dog active or competing in sports? Dogs that get a great deal of exercise require a diet that provides them with the nutrition and energy they need. Generally you'll have two choices: active adult or performance formula.

Most moderately active dogs can get by with an active adult formula. However, if you're working your dog three or more times a week, you'll want to consider a performance formula. If your dog is regularly active in agility, flyball, hunting, sledding, herding, and other equally demanding activities, you'll definitely want him on a performance food. If your dog only participates in such activities infrequently, he will be fine on active adult food.

If your dog is losing weight, lacks energy even when fit, or suffers sprains or other injuries, you should switch him to a performance formula. If he is rapidly gaining weight on a performance food, you should switch him back to active adult dog food.

How much do you feed? Most of your dog's food will have to be gauged according to his activity and fitness level. To some extent, common sense applies. If he is skin and bones, then feeding more is better. If he's an infamous "ribless dog"—and I've seen several, even when competing—you need to cut back or go with an active adult formula.

© *Margaret H. Bonham*

Sled dogs require extra energy they can't quite get in dog food.

Feeding Sled Dogs: A Whole Other Concept

Sled dog nutrition violates everything I've said up to now. There is no sport more demanding than sled dog racing. Sled dogs frequently burn in excess of 7,000 calories a day; top Iditarod dogs, when racing, burn over 10,000 calories a day. To put that in perspective, a person weighing 150 pounds would have to eat 30,000 to 40,000 calories a day to burn as much as a 50-pound sled dog. That's a lot!

Optimal Requirements for Sled Dogs

Sled dogs require 50 to 65 percent of their caloric intake from fat, 30 to 35 percent of their caloric intake from protein, and only 10 to 15 percent of their caloric intake from carbohydrates. Note that these are caloric percentages, not dry matter, so when you look at the labels, you'll need to convert to caloric percentages. (See Chapter 13 for more information on how to convert caloric percentages.)

Consult a veterinary nutritionist when developing your own sled dog diet.

How to Mix It Up

Because of the higher percentages of fat and protein sled dogs require, their diets require supplementation. The good news is that
there are meat supplements formulated for sled dogs to provide the
correct balance, most notably the Champaign Diet. This diet was
developed by famous sprint sled dog racer Charlie Champaign, and
is made to mix with a premium dog food. The bad news is that the
Champaign Diet isn't available everywhere. Other frozen meat formulas might work to bring the performance food up to requirements,
but you have to make sure you
maintain the right protein/fat/
carbohydrate ratio.

There are powdered and dehydrated forms of meat substitutes
available as well. These substitutes
are intended to be mixed with the
dog food and do not provide complete and balanced nutrition by
themselves.

> **Dog Treats**
> Two books that offer
> sled dog diets are *The Speed
> Mushing Manual* by Jim Welch
> (Sirius Publishing, 1989) and
> *The Secrets of Long Distance
> Training and Racing* by Rick
> Swenson (L&B Color Printing,
> 1987).

Another way to maintain your sled dog's diet is to mix your own food. This requires meat, fat, vitamins and mineral supplements, eggs, dog food, wheat germ oil, brewer's yeast, and other ingredients. It's expensive and requires some serious knowledge of dog nutrition and lots of freezer space. You should consult a veterinary nutritionist who is familiar with sled dog nutrition to help you create the right diet for your dogs.

Food Analysis

If you do concoct a sled dog diet, you must have it analyzed. Because sled dogs depend so much on their nutrition, a mistake will be very costly and could adversely affect the health of the entire team. Most veterinary universities can run feed analyses through their large animal college. You'll want to check the percentages of protein, fat, and carbohydrates, as well as do a mineral analysis.

© Margaret H. Bonham

Small-breed dogs may require more protein while growing.

The Least You Need to Know

- Select your dog food according to the age, activity level, and fitness of your dog, taking into consideration any health concerns.

- Choose a puppy food according to your puppy's weight and activity level. Some offer specialized breed formulas. Feed your puppy three to four times a day if he is younger than 6 months old.

- Choose an adult dog food according to your dog's weight and activity level. Feed your adult dog two to three times a day.

- Active dogs will do fine on either an active dog or performance dog food.

- Don't switch your senior dog to a senior dog food unless he is inactive and gaining weight.

- Most active dogs do well on an active adult formula, however, if your dog is losing weight or getting injured, consider switching to a performance version of the dog food.

- Very active dogs, that is, dogs that participate in sports, require a premium performance blend.

- Sled dogs are the top canine athletes and require a higher percentage of protein and fat than even premium performance can give. Supplementation is usually required for competitive sled dogs.

Glossary

allopathic   Conventional medicine.

amino acids   Building blocks that make up protein.

ash   General term for the residue (total mineral content) remaining after a dog food has been tested in the laboratory through burning.

autoimmune disorders   Disorders in which the dog's body produces an immune system response so often that it begins producing an immune system response for conditions that are not disease.

calorie   A calorie is a measure of energy. It is the energy required to raise the temperature of a gram of water by 1° Centigrade.

carpal   Bones in the wrists.

chemotherapy   The treatment of a disease with medications or chemicals.

colostrum   The milk produced by the mother during the first 24 hours after her puppies are born.

complete and balanced   A statement meaning that the dog food is nutritionally complete.

complete protein source   A source of protein that contains all 10 essential amino acids.

congenital   A condition that is present at birth that may have either genetic or environmental causes.

digestibility   The percentage of your dog's food that he metabolizes rather than eliminates.

double coat   A coat with an undercoat that adds extra insulation.

dry-matter basis   The percentage or amount of nutrient as compared to the overall weight of the dog food without water.

essential amino acids   Amino acids that must be present in a dog's diet to prevent a deficiency.

glycogen   A type of fuel used by a cell.

hereditary   A condition that is genetic, that is, inherited through the genes of the parents.

holistic   Medical treatment that considers the whole animal instead of simply treating the symptoms.

idiopathic   A disease or condition whose cause is unknown.

immune system response   The production of antibodies against a disease.

incomplete protein source   A source of protein that contains only nine or less of the essential amino acids.

kilocalorie   A kilocalorie is the energy required to raise the temperature of a kilogram of water by 1° Centigrade.

lymphoma   Cancer of the lymphatic system.

microfilariae   Heartworm larvae that infect a dog.

modality   A form or mode of treatment.

nonessential amino acids   Amino acids that are manufactured within a dog's body.

novel protein   A protein that is new or normally not fed in a diet.

nutriceuticals   A form of supplementation using natural substances or a nutritional supplement intended to help mitigate a condition or disease.

polygenic   A trait or condition that comes from more than one gene pair.

Pyometra   A life-threatening condition in which the female dog's uterus becomes infected.

quick   The portion of a dog's nail with blood vessels that supply the nail.

radiation therapy   The treatment of a disease with radiation.

radius   Bone in the forelegs (front legs) between the elbow and wrists.

sarcoma   A malignant tumor.

single coat   A coat that is similar to human hair, that is, it has no undercoat.

succusion   The process of diluting and mixing homeopathic medicine.

titer   The level and strength of antibodies in a dog.

wellness care   Another term for preventative care.

Organizations

Agility Association of Canada (AAC)
RR #2
Lucan, Ontario
N0N2J0
519-657-7636

Alaska Skijoring & Pulk Association (Skijoring/Pulka)
P.O. Box 82843
Fairbanks, AK 99708
e-mail: bunky@cagle.ptialaska.net
website: www.sleddog.org/skijor

AKC Companion Animal Recovery
5580 Centerview Drive, Suite 250
Raleigh, NC 27606-3389
1-800-252-7894
website: www.akccar.org

American Animal Hospital Association (AAHA)
P.O. Box 150899
Denver, CO 80215-0899
1-800-252-2242
website: www.aahanet.org

American College of Veterinary Internal Medicine
1997 Wadsworth Boulevard, Suite A
Lakewood, CO 80215-3327
1-800-245-9081
website: www.acvim.org

American Holistic Veterinary Medical Association
2214 Old Emmorton Road
Bel Air, MD 21015
410-569-0795

American Kennel Club (AKC)
5580 Centerview Drive
Raleigh, NC 27606-3390
919-233-9767
e-mail: info@akc.org
website: www.akc.org

American Veterinary Chiropractic Association
P.O. Box 249
Port Byron, IL 61275
309-523-3995

American Veterinary Medical Association
1931 N. Meacham Road, Suite 100
Schaumburg, IL 60173-4360
847-925-8070
website: www.avma.org

Canine Backpackers Association LLC (Hiking and Backpacking)
P.O. Box 934
Conifer, CO 80433
website: www.caninebackpackers.org

Canine Eye Registration Foundation (CERF)
Department of Veterinary Clinical Science
School of Veterinary Medicine

Purdue University
West Lafayette, IN 47907
765-494-8179
website: www.vet.purdue.edu/~yshen/cerf.html

Canine Freestyle Federation
Monica Patty, Corresponding Secretary
21900 Foxden Lane
Leesburg, VA 20175
e-mail: secretary@canine-freestyle.org
website: www.canine-freestyle.org

Flying Disc Dog Open©
Bill Watters/Director
P.O. Box 4615
Cave Creek, Arizona 85327
1-888-383 3357
480-595-0580 in Arizona
website: www.airmajorsdoghouse.com/fddo/

International Federation of Sled Dog Sports (IFSS) (Skijoring)
Maureen Nicholls, IFSS Secretary General
Prospect House
Charlton
Kilmersdon
Bath, England BA3 5TN
e-mail: secretary.ifss@ukonline.co.uk
website: www.antenna-media.com/worldsport/sports/
sleddog/home.html

International Sled Dog Racing Association (Skijoring)
HC 86, Box 3390
Merrifield, MN 56465
phone: 218-765-4297
e-mail: dsteele@brainerd.net
website: www.isdra.org

International Veterinary Acupuncture Society (IVAS)
P.O. Box 1478
Longmont, CO 80534
303-682-1167

National Canine Air Champions (NCAC)
The Washington D.C. Area Frisbee Disc Dog Club
2830 Meadow Lane
Falls Church, VA 22042
703-532-0709
website: www.discdog.com

National Center for Homeopathy
801 N. Fairfax #306
Alexandria, VA 22314
703-548-7790

National Dog Groomers Association of America
P.O. Box 101
Clark, PA 16113
724-962-2711
e-mail: ndga@nauticom.net

National Dog Registry
P.O. Box 116
Woodstock, NY 12498
1-800-637-3647
website: www.natldogregistry.com

North American Dog Agility Council (NADAC)
HCR 2, Box 277
St. Maries, ID 83861
208-689-3803
e-mail: nadack9@aol.com
website: http://www.nadac.com/

North American Flyball Association, Inc.
1400 W. Devon Avenue, #512
Chicago, IL 60660
309-688-9840
e-mail: flyball@flyball.org
website: www.flyballdogs.com/flyball.html

Orthopedic Foundation for Animals (OFA)
2300 Nifong Boulevard
Columbia, MO 65201
573-442-0418
website: www.offa.org

PennHIP
Synbiotics Corporation
11011 Via Frontera
San Diego, CA 92127
858-451-3771
website: www.synbiotics.com/html/chd_penn_hip.html

Pet Assure
10 S. Morris Street
Dover, NJ 07801
1-888-789-PETS (7387)
e-mail: custserv@petassure.com
website: www.petassure.com

PetCare Insurance Programs
P.O. Box 8575
Rolling Meadows, IL 60008-8575
1-866-275-PETS (7387)
e-mail: info@petcareinsurance.com
website: www.petcareinsurance.com/us

Pet Plan Insurance (Canada)
777 Portage Avenue
Winnipeg, CANADA MB R3G 0N3
905-279-7190
website: www.petplan.com

Petshealth Insurance Agency
P.O. Box 2847
Canton, OH 44720
1-888-592-7387
website: www.petshealthplan.com

Premier Pet Insurance Group
9541 Harding Boulevard
Wauwatosa, WI 53226
1-877-774-2273
website: www.ppins.com

Skyhoundz
4060 Peachtree Road, Suite D #326
Atlanta, GA 30319
404-256-4513
e-mail: info@skyhoundz.com
website: www.skyhoundz.com/

Tattoo-A-Pet
6571 S.W. 20th Court
Ft. Lauderdale, FL 33317
1-800-828-8667
website: www.tattoo-a-pet.com

United Kennel Club (UKC)
100 East Kilgore Road
Kalamazoo, MI 49001-5593
website: www.ukcdogs.com

United States Dog Agility Association (USDAA)
P.O. Box 850955
Richardson, TX 75085-0955
972-231-9700
Information Line: 1-888–AGILITY
e-mail: info@usdaa.com
website: www.usdaa.com

Veterinary Pet Insurance (VPI)
P.O. Box 2344
Brea, CA 92822-2344
1-800-USA-PETS
website: www.petinsurance.com

World Canine Freestyle Organization, Ltd.
P.O. Box 250122
Brooklyn, NY 11235
718-332-8336
Fax: 718-646-2686
e-mail: wcfodogs@aol.com
website: www.worldcaninefreestyle.org

Appendix **C**

Periodicals and Books

Periodicals

AKC Gazette
51 Madison Avenue
New York, NY 10010
website: www.akc.org

Dog Fancy Magazine
P.O. Box 53264
Boulder, CO 80322-3264
1-800-365-4421
website: www.dogfancy.com

Dog World
P.O. Box 56240
Boulder, CO 80323-6240
1-800-361-8056
website: www.dogworld.com

Books

Alderton, David. *The Dog Care Manual.* Hauppauge, NY: Barron's Educational Series, 1986.

American Kennel Club. *The Complete Dog Book.* 19th ed. rev. New York: Howell Book House, 1997.

Benjamin, Carol Lea. *Second-Hand Dog.* New York, NY: Howell Book House, 1988.

Bonham, Margaret H. *An Introduction to Dog Agility.* Hauppauge, NY: Barron's Educational Series, 2000.

———. *The Simple Guide to Getting Active with Your Dog.* Neptune City, NJ: TFH Publications Inc., 2002.

Brennan, Mary L., with Norma Eckroate. *The Natural Dog.* New York, NY: Plume Books, 1994.

Coffman, Howard D. *The Dry Dog Food Reference.* Nashua, NH: Pig Dog Press, 1995.

Elliot, Rachel Page. *The New Dogsteps.* New York, NY: Howell Book House, 1983.

Giffin, James M., M.D., and Liisa D. Carlson, D.V.M., *The Dog Owner's Home Veterinary Handbook.* 3rd ed. New York, NY: Howell Book House, 2000.

Gilbert, Edward M. Jr., and Thelma R. Brown. *K-9 Structure and Terminology.* New York, NY: Howell Book House, 1995.

Hinchcliff, Kenneth W. B.V.Sc., M.S., Ph.D., Diplomate ACVIM, Gregory A. Reinhart, Ph.D., and Arleigh J. Reynolds. *Performance Dog Nutrition.* Dayton, OH: The Iams Company, 1999.

Holst, Phyllis A., M.S., D.V.M. *Canine Reproduction, A Breeder's Guide*. Loveland, CO: Alpine Publications, 1985.

James, Ruth B., D.V.M. *The Dog Repair Book*. Mills, WY: Alpine Press, 1990.

Klever, Ulrich. *The Complete Book of Dog Care*. Hauppauge, NY: Barron's Educational Series, 1989.

LaBelle, Charlene. *A Guide to Backpacking with Your Dog*. Loveland, CO: Alpine Publications, 1993.

Merck and Co. *The Merck Veterinary Manual*. 7th ed. Whitehouse Station, NJ: Merck and Co, Inc., 1991.

Ralston Purina Company. *Purina's Complete Guide to Nutrition, Care, and Health for Your Dog and Cat*. St. Louis, MO.

Streitferdt, Uwe. *Healthy Dog, Happy Dog*. Hauppauge, NY: Barron's Educational Series, 1994.

Volhard, Joachim, Wendy Volhard, and Jack Volhard. *The Canine Good Citizen: Every Dog Can Be One*. New York: Howell Book House, 1997.

Volhard, Wendy, and Kerry Brown. *The Holistic Guide for a Healthy Dog*. New York, NY: Howell Book House, 1995.

Zink, M. Chris D.V.M., Ph.D. *Peak Performance: Coaching the Canine Athlete*. New York, NY: Howell Book House, 1992.

Index

E

skin. *See also* coats
  excessive scratching, 112
  health exams, 32
skunk sprays, remedies, 114
sled dogs, feeding guidelines
  Champaign Diets, 263
  food analysis, 264
  optimal requirements, 262
small breed dog foods
  adult dogs, 258
  puppies, 256
snacks
  Cheese Bone Cookies, 190
  dog biscuit recipe, 188
  feeding recommendations, 189
sodium, 205
spaying, 28-30
  health and behavior benefits, 30
  myths, 28
special formulated diets, 260
  allergy diets, 236-237
  cancer diets, 237
  diabetic diets, 237
  heart diets, 238
  intestinal and pancreatic diets, 238
  kidney diets, 238
  liver diets, 238
  recovery diets, 238
  urinary diets, 238-239
  weight management diets, 239
sports (dog sports), 54
  agility
    classes and clubs, 58
    contact obstacles, 57
    Jumpers Class, 57
    Jumpers with Weaves, 57
    Standard Class, 57
    USDAA (United States Dog Agility Association), 56
    weave poles, 57
  backpacking, 58-59
    equipment, 59
    weight restrictions, 59

flyball
  clubs and competitions, 60
  equipment, 60-61
flying disc, 61-62
freestyle dancing, 62
skijoring
  equipment, 63
  requirements, 63
  suppliers, 64
Springer Rage, 149
Standard Class (agility), 57
stings, 139-140
Sub-Aortic Stenosis. *See* SAS
succusion, 81-82
supplements, 192
  puppies, 256
  sled dog diets, 263
support groups, pet loss support groups, 98
surgical techniques, cancer treatments, 92

T

table scraps, feeding recommendations, 190
tags (identification tags), 33
tails, health exams, 32
tapeworms, 119
tattoo identification, 34-35
technological advancements in veterinary care
  cancer treatments, 91-94
    chemotherapy, 93
    diagnostics, 92
    radiation therapy, 93
    surgical techniques, 92
    vaccinations, 93-94
  epilepsy treatments, 94-95
  vaccinations, 90
teeth
  brushing, 47
  signs of tooth and gum problems, 47

W–X–Y–Z